The Wild Woman

The Wild Woman:
An Inquiry into the
Anthropology of an Idea

by

Sharon W. Tiffany and Kathleen J. Adams

Schenkman Publishing Company, Inc.
Cambridge, Massachusetts

Cover Source: *Legends and Myths of the Aboriginal Indians of British Guiana,* edited by Reverend William H. Brett (London: William Wells Gardner, 1880).

© 1985 by Sharon W. Tiffany and Kathleen J. Adams.
All rights reserved.

HQ 1121
.T46
1985

Library of Congress Cataloging in Publication Data

Tiffany, Sharon W.
   The wild woman.

   Bibliography: p.
   Includes index. History
   1. Women—Historiography. 2. Sex role—Historiography.
   3. Matriarchy—Historiography. I. Adams, Kathleen J.
   II. Title.
   GN479.7.T5 1984   305.4'0722   84-22161
   ISBN 0-87073-243-9
   ISBN 0-87073-213-7 (pbk.)

Printed in the United States of America

All rights reserved. This book, or parts thereof,
may not be reproduced in any form without written
permission from the publisher.

One wonders if women still exist, if they will always exist, whether or not it is desirable that they should, what place they occupy in this world, what their place should be.

Simone de Beauvoir, *The Second Sex*

Contents

Acknowledgments	ix
Introduction	xi
1. The Archaic Matriarch	1
Observing the Observers	4
Anthropological Monologues	4
The Science of Man Studies the Wild Woman	7
Woman Evolving	7
The Persistence of Matriarchal Ideas	10
The Lady and the Savage	12
Body as Woman	15
Mother as Victim	19
2. Encounters with the Wild Woman	23
The Wild Woman as Victim	24
Trouble in Paradise	25
The Civilized and the Savage	29
The Wild Woman as Man-Eater	32
The Nightshade of Pacific Nether Worlds	33
The Wild Woman in Anthropology	35
3. The Primitive Woman	39
The Nuer: Women's Place in an African Society	40
The Problem of the Wild Woman	40
Bridewealth and the Exchange of Women	43
Social Order and Women's "Station"	45

The Australian Tiwi: Games Savages Play	47
Mothers and Wives in Polygynous Marriages	48
Women and Politics in the Australian Outback	49
Rage and Rape among the Amazonian Yanomama	51
Victims and Victimizers in the Tropics	53
4. The Virgin and the Amazon	61
America as Woman	62
The Torrid Zone	63
Sexual License and Utopia in the New World	67
Guyana as Unexplored Virgin	69
Walter Raleigh's Maid	69
The Hidden Amazon	71
The Rain Forest and the Fecund Mother	76
Zoological Exotica	77
Women as Flora and Fauna	80
The Primeval Woman Within	84
The Hidden World of Wild Women	84
The Mother-Monster	91
5. The Romance Revisited	97
Female Terrain	99
Person as Woman	101
Notes	103
Bibliography	109
Index	145

Acknowledgments

We are grateful for the support of Marilyn Enstad, Harold A. Freeman, and Walter W. Tiffany. Our publisher, the late Alfred S. Schenkman, remained committed to this book during the several years of its development.

Many colleagues have assisted us. We especially thank Jane Goodale and Jacques Lizot. Their detailed commentaries on the Tiwi and the Yanomama, among whom they respectively conducted fieldwork, greatly enriched our analysis, for which we alone are responsible.

We dedicate this book to the women of Samoa and of the Guyanese rain forest. In many ways, during fieldwork and afterward, they helped us form the ideas presented here.

Permission to quote from the following works is gratefully acknowledged:

Prentice-Hall, Inc.: Eric R. Wolf, *Anthropology* (Englewood Cliffs, New Jersey: Prentice-Hall, 1964), p. 12. Copyright © by Eric R. Wolf. Reprinted by permission of the author.

Random House, Inc.: Adrienne Rich, "Foreword. Conditions for Work: The Common World of Women," in *Working It Out: Twenty-Three Women Writers, Artists, Scientists, and Scholars Talk about Their Lives and Work*, eds. Sara Ruddick and Pamela Daniels (New York: Random House, Pantheon Books, 1977), p. xv. Copyright © by Adrienne Rich. Reprinted by permission of the author.

Random House, Inc.: Simone de Beauvoir, *The Second Sex*, trans. and ed. by H. M. Parshley (New York: Random House, Vintage Books, 1952), p. xv. Reprinted by permission of Random House, Inc.

Introduction: An Invitation to the Romance of the Wild Woman

Men find women a mystery: women's actions are equivocal—their sexual desires a puzzle. Idealized as morally and spiritually superior to men, women are, alternately, denigrated as biologically and socially inferior. These ideas about women parallel the Western imagination of primitive peoples. Like women, primitives suffer the jeopardy of being simultaneously superior and inferior to civilized men. Primitives live simple lives in remote places; their childish "superstitions" and "bizarre" customs, particularly their sexual behavior, make no sense to the modern mind. By this logic, civilized men are sophisticated, women and primitives are naive; civilized men are rational, women and primitives rely on magic and ritual; and civilized men abide by social restraints, women and primitives are uninhibited.

In their search for the primitive, anthropologists have succeeded in reinforcing this contrast to Western men's lives. Like peoples of the non-West, women are the losers in these invidious comparisons. Women, the archetype of what men are not, provide the focus of a political inequality that is general among men. Appearing in various roles as Amazons, virgins, and matriarchs, women represent a projection of civilized men's imaginations. This book is about images of women and an idea; we call it the Romance of the Wild Woman.

Just as the Wild Woman was invented, so too was the

exotic, the primitive, and the Third World. Like "developing" regions of the world and the peoples within them, the Wild Woman conveys images of submission to exploitation—images translated into concrete relations of sex and power that confront women everywhere.

Written in the spirit of feminist commitment and inquiry, this book demystifies the Wild Woman. To trace the romance back in time will enable us to comprehend what has so far remained unnamed and, therefore, compelling. We discard female nature as essentially wild and take a step toward claiming our own identities.

Our commitment to feminism encourages us to use our anthropological skills reflexively, to study the idea of the Wild Woman in order to combat its psychic and social consequences for women. We use our understanding of culture to investigate a romance shared by many—natural historians, explorers, geographers, missionaries, adventurers, novelists, and anthropologists—those who claim the right to observe and evaluate other peoples and lands. The history of the Romance of the Wild Woman shows the tenacious power of this idea, as Westerners continue the quest for their versions of truth in strange terrains inhabited by Wild Women.

This book is addressed to an audience concerned about the lives and experiences of women everywhere. We perceive our task to be stimulating criticism and debate, and we challenge others to pursue additional research on the legacy of the Wild Woman.

1. The Archaic Matriarch

In a world where language and naming are power, silence is oppression, is violence.[1]

Adrienne Rich, 1977

This book is about an idea and its consequences for women. We call this idea the Romance of the Wild Woman, a constellation of images, metaphors, and meanings about women and their sexuality set against the contrast between civilization and the primitive. Rooted in Western civilization and ideas, the romance extends back in time to classical antiquity. Pythagorean oppositions between male and female and Aristotelian discourses on sex and gender differences focused on the problematic nature of womankind. According to this intellectual legacy, framed in androcentric language, women *make* problems and women *are* problems.

The problematic nature of women is connected to several questions concerning biology, sexuality, motherhood, and domesticity—recurrent issues in the history of political philosophy and in contemporary scientific thinking about sex, gender, and the social order. The problems that women are thought to pose for society in general, and men in particular, are cast into scientific controversies about the public versus the private domain, as nature versus culture, or as reason versus emotion. Women are the passive contrasts in these oppositions—the objects to be intellectually and scientifically acted upon. Described as closer to nature and reproductively chained to the domestic, women are contrasted with men, the cultural innovators actively involved with the public concerns of society. Biologically enjoined to follow their feminine intuition, women are considered bereft of objectivity and reason—attributes exclusively in the domain of men. The ideas and images about women conveyed in these vocabularies of sexual contrast have significantly influenced our understanding of the human condition, both past and present.[2]

Feminism seeks to identify the covert assumptions about women that issue from the knowledge generated by men. As the growing feminist scholarship demonstrates, anthropologists have also begun to examine their discipline in response to feminist criticisms. Revising anthropological knowledge about women requires reflexive scrutiny and evaluation of the tools that both anthropological and feminist inquiry provide.[3]

Commonly referred to as the "Science of Man," anthropology is ideally concerned with the comparative study of Mankind in the generic sense of the term. In practice, however, the Science of Man has been, and continues to be, concerned with men and their understandings of social relations.

Anthropologists evaluate human behavior in a language that silences and dismisses women. The following statement about the fieldwork enterprise illustrates how women are transformed into muted, faceless others:

> The fact is that no one could come back from an ethnographic study of 'the X', having talked only *to* women *about* men, without professional comment and some self-doubt. The reverse can and does happen constantly. (Ardener 1972:138, emphasis in original)

The invisibility of women in anthropology reflects the exclusion of feminist issues. Women are not people; they are commodities, objects of exchange who do not speak for themselves.

The consequences *for* women of anthropological knowledge *about* women are the suppression of women's participation in social life. As one anthropologist concluded,

> One gets the impression from many ethnographies that culture is created by and for men between the ages of puberty and late middle age, with children, women, and the aged as residual categories; women are frequently portrayed, at best, as providing support for the activities of men. (Schlegel 1977:2)

Analyzing the processes that trivialize and silence women is critical in feminist inquiry. Silencing women renders them powerless and reduces their roles in their own societies. Therefore, we must question the entire corpus of anthropological knowledge of the human experience because it is knowledge based on male experiences and the acceptance of men's power to articulate for those who are not allowed to speak for themselves.[4]

As feminists we criticize androcentric anthropology while recognizing that the discipline of anthropology is a core concern of feminist theory. The reasons are fundamental. The anthropological perspective is worldwide and comparative, encompassing all peoples, cultures, histories, and regions. Anthropology emphasizes comparative understanding of oneself and one's society by observing the public and private worlds of others. Students of the Western world therefore look to anthropologists as interpreters of exotic others, who serve as explicit contrasts to the Western self. Anthropologists write and speak *about* and, to a large extent, continue to write and speak *for* peoples of the Third, or Other World. Our goals, as feminist anthropologists, are to understand these other worlds and to confront male-defined domains of the mind and social life.

In this chapter, we examine the Romance of the Wild Woman in primitive and civilized worlds. We introduce the ways anthropologists have used the romance in their cross-cultural research, and in the next sections we explore the convergence of these ideas in the anthropology of other worlds with those of the West.

OBSERVING THE OBSERVERS

Anthropology is cast within the domain of scientific objectivity—a domain that accepts human relationships as male-oriented and male-dominated. Androcentric vocabularies inform anthropological discourse about women. An intimate relation thus exists between the Romance of the Wild Woman and the anthropological study of exotic others.

Anthropological Monologues

Contrasts between civilized and savage, white and black, East and West, and, more recently, developed and underdeveloped, are important themes in Western ideas. Anthropology is an integral part of this intellectual and political legacy. Observers of the exotic—explorers, traders, adventurers, missionaries, soldiers, and colonial officers—have been largely superseded by anthropologists. Early observers interpreted the foreign in vocabularies meaningful to Western experiences and interests; anthropologists continue to do so.

Anthropology adds a unique dimension to the study of the foreign. At best, anthropologists attempt to achieve a comparative understanding of human experiences and aspirations in past and present societies—societies that differ radically from what Westerners perceive as their own civilized and orderly world. To acquire this comprehension, the anthropological researcher must first collect "data" by relating to informants, people who provide information about their own culture. In order to generate understandings of the "native other," the anthropologist as outsider interacts with and collects information about the society under study from the indigenous insider. This method of field research is known as participant-observation.

The role of participant-observer is ambiguous. As temporary stranger and socially powerful outsider, the anthropologist seeks intimacy with those persons being observed. The participant-observer role itself should lead to a scrutiny of the anthropological enterprise—a scrutiny few have dared to undertake. The researcher's understandings about the native other, selected and eventually disseminated in the published literature as anthropological knowledge, rest upon a "cultural baggage" of unquestioned presumptions. The assumptions that shape the anthropologist's interpretations of others' behaviors and motives remain hidden beneath the bedrock of ethnographic data.

Despite its promise of comparative understanding, conventional anthropological inquiry is, in fact, a one-sided discourse in which the researcher-observer engages in monologue. At worst, conclusions about the observed may rest on little more than what the anthropologist expected to see. In such instances, the observed are interpreted within and conform to the unexamined premises and preconceptions of the observer.

This practice highlights the relations of asymmetry between the observing self and the observed other: The more powerful are privy to describe; the less powerful are described. In this monologue, the observer is not observed. The anthropological enterprise assumes that its own practitioners, without seriously examining their own values and culturally based assumptions, can objectively know others. The active self perceives and interprets; the passive other behaves and submits. The more powerful is unchallenged and unknown, yet intimately "understands" others. The anthropologist thus presumes to be an objective arbiter of the social and existential realities of others.[5]

Primitive and Modern Mirrors. Two forefathers in the history of anthropology understood the significance of self-reflection. In charting the scope of the anthropological enterprise, Franz Boas ([1928] 1962:11) insisted on self-review:

> Anthropology is often considered a collection of curious facts, telling about the peculiar appearance of exotic people and describing their strange customs and beliefs. It is looked upon as an entertaining diversion, apparently without any bearing upon the conduct of life of civilized communities.

> This opinion is mistaken.... [A] clear understanding of the principles of anthropology illuminates the social processes of our own times and may show us, if we are ready to listen to its teachings, what to do and what to avoid.

Contrasts between the known and the unfamiliar invite self-reflection. Uncivilized or primitive others—their "peculiar appearance" and "strange customs and beliefs"—provide the mirror in which we perceive ourselves. The anthropological study of others, then, implies contrasts. Without the civilized there is no savage or primitive.

Similarly, the self is understood in reference to the other. In his classic book, *The Primitive World and Its Transformations*, Robert Redfield (1953:84–110) used the term "world view" to compare the primitive and the modern. He described world view as

> the way we see ourselves in relation to all else. Every world view is a stage set. On that stage myself is an important character; in every world view there is an "I" from which the view is taken. On the stage are other people, toward whom the view is directed. (Redfield 1953:86)

Redfield conceived the primitive world by contrasting it to the modern. Yet a chasm of inequality separates these two worlds. This political asymmetry is manifested in the interaction between researcher and informant.[6] The epistemological consequences that flow from this relationship reinforce the cultural baggage of values and ideas carried by the anthropologist.

Androcentric vocabularies are part of that baggage. Submerged in the discourse of anthropology is the separation of self from other. The literature of anthropology conveys this separation by an implicit simplification of other worlds portrayed as primitive and submissive. Geographic distance carries a diminished evaluation of faraway places—places associated in the Western imagination with primal nature and untamed wilderness. Similarly, peoples of these distant lands are considered children of nature or wild savages. The

Romance of the Wild Woman condenses these contradictory images of foreign peoples, particularly women, as catalogued entries in popular and in anthropological literature.

Our interest in this book concerns the ideological and social processes of dehumanization that occur when women everywhere are viewed as Wild Women. Categorized as exotica in male-dominated social worlds, women of Western and non-Western cultures are transposed into the Wild Woman, an inhabitant of the uncharted domain of nature.

THE SCIENCE OF MAN STUDIES THE WILD WOMAN

Despite the presumption of value-neutrality, male-dominated science is frequently caught up in the political issues and social policies of the day. For example, nineteenth-century evolutionists and twentieth-century eugenicists viewed with alarm feminist redefinitions of women's reproductive and domestic roles. Scientists saw these revisions as serious threats to the structure of society. Terms of scientific inquiry have shifted from nature and nurture to genes and gender, but the debate about women is essentially the same.[7]

Woman Evolving

Evolutionary theories of the nineteenth century addressed the problem of women, a debate that also shaped the emerging discipline of anthropology. Evolutionists classified the entire history of social development into three universal stages: savagery, barbarism, and civilization. Savage society was contrasted with civilized society, which represented the apex of industrial progress. Savagery and barbarism—associated with sexual promiscuity, Amazon revolts, and matriarchy—would eventually culminate in civilization associated with a male vision of women's submission to a patriarchal social order. Such male-dominated values, which attained their definition in Victorian idioms, continue to find expression in contemporary anthropology.

Evolutionism was fraught with contradictions. It assumed progressive changes in the domestic and reproductive roles of women—changes that liberated women of civilized society from the burdens of overwork, sexual abuse, and male violence associated with the lot of savage and barbaric women. Evolutionary anthropologists therefore promoted change for these women in the name of progress, but justified the *status quo* of civilized Victorian women of middle- and upper-class backgrounds by arguing that further changes would be deleterious to the entire social fabric (Duffin 1978:57–59). Primitive women living in a brutish state of nature could therefore aspire to the benefits civilization bestowed upon the "weaker sex," while Victorian women who already enjoyed these privileges were expected to be content with their place. Evolutionary ideas, then, allowed the possibility for primitive women to escape from male exploitation by aspiring to the ideals of Victorian womanhood. Primitive women could become imperfect imitations of Victorian women, who themselves were locked into their prescribed roles as mothers and moral guardians.

The Primal Mother. Evolutionary debates followed a common theme about the problem of women. As a Swiss jurist, Johann Bachofen (1861) wrote with authority. His paradigm was an elaborate version of the matriarch's early role in shaping society during the barbaric stage of development. Women triumphed over men in barbarous societies by domesticating them; matriarchy thus became "a sign of cultural progress" (Bachofen [1861] 1967:91). The development of patriarchal institutions eventually subverted women's roles as mothers and civilizers in matriarchal societies. Recognizing the legitimacy of paternity resulted in the debasement of maternity. Motherhood was relegated to the animal, savage world:

> The triumph of paternity brings with it the liberation of the spirit from the manifestations of nature, a sublimation of human existence over the laws of material life. While the principle of motherhood is

common to all spheres of tellurian [earthly] life, man, by the preponderant position he accords to the begetting potency, emerges from this relationship and becomes conscious of his higher calling. Spiritual life rises over corporeal existence, and the relation with the lower spheres of existence is restricted to the physical aspect. Maternity pertains to the physical side of man, the only thing he shares with the animals. (Bachofen [1861] 1967:109)

Biology discredits the matriarch, whereas men sublimate their urges and come to dominate women and society.

Like other evolutionists of his day, Bachofen interpreted the development of matriarchy in sexual terms. The primitive woman sought to entrap men by controlling their access to her sexuality and by forcing them to support her children. Matriarchy epitomized the nakedly overt rule of women over men. Bachofen further assumed that the ancient stage of matriarchy, with women in ascendancy, was still to be found in Asia and Africa. For evolutionary theorists, matriarchy highlighted the importance of women as mothers and domesticators—depoliticized ideals embellished in the nineteenth-century model of Victorian womanhood.

Matriarchal women subdued men, but not for long. The evolutionary transition from matriarchy to patriarchy, it was argued, broke the female monopoly of ritual and sexual power. "Higher" concerns of male intellect and creativity subordinated the female principles of fertility and procreation. Thus men forged civilized society by conquering the matriarch.

According to evolutionism, Victorian women retained their animal natures, despite their veneer of domesticity. Moreover, there was no place for the civilized woman to go, except backward. Yielding to the passions inherent in female nature constituted downfall. The sullied reputation of the "fallen" Victorian woman was irreparable.

As a legacy of these ideas, women are perceived as biological and social relics. Bound to nature by maternity, women are breeders and nurturers. As domesticators, they are left behind from the course of civilization. Women are in charge of their children and of their own sexuality, which must be contained. Men oversee both processes.

The Persistence of Matriarchal Ideas

By the early decades of the twentieth century, evolutionary stages of worldwide human development, along with matriarchy as a form of social organization in which women dominated men, were discredited in the anthropological literature. Nonetheless, the evolutionists' legacy of ideas about matriarchy and patriarchy continued. Women are repeatedly described as sexual and parturient and men as innovators and achievers. Not surprisingly, matriarchal ideas about gender, sex, and power stir considerable interest among feminists.[8]

Charlotte Perkins Gilman, an early modern feminist, recognized the persistence of matriarchal ideas and their attraction. She adapted these ideas for a feminist audience. In her utopian novel *Herland* (1915), Gilman explored matriarchal ideas, utilizing the theme of powerful and resourceful women who live without men. Set in the tropical unknown, this "strange and terrible Woman Land in the high distance" is recreated in the minds of three men who seek to find it after listening to the bizarre stories recounted by their savage, unlettered guides:

> None of them had ever seen it. It was dangerous, deadly, they said, for any man to go there. But there were tales of long ago, when some brave investigator had seen it—a Big Country, Big Houses, Plenty People—All Women. (Gilman [1915] 1979:2–3)

The primitive female in matriarchal worlds lurks and waits for the man crazy or brash enough to pursue her. The male attempt to discredit and eventually subdue the matriarchal vision is a recurrent theme in *Herland*. "There was," Gilman ([1915] 1979:5) wrote, "something attractive to a bunch of unattached young men in finding an undiscovered country of a strictly Amazonian nature."

Gilman's novel highlighted men's incredulity that matriarchal women could be cooperative and responsible. The three adventurers speculate about what an all-female society is like:

> "They would fight among themselves," Terry insisted. "Women always do. We mustn't look to find any sort of order and organization."
>
> "You're dead wrong," Jeff told him. "It will be like a nunnery under an abbess—a peaceful, harmonious sisterhood."
>
> I [Van, the friend of Terry and Jeff] snorted derision at this idea.
>
> "Nuns, indeed! Your peaceful sisterhoods were all celibate, Jeff, and under vows of obedience. These are just women, and mothers, and where there's motherhood you don't find sisterhood—not much."
>
> "No, sir—they'll scrap," agreed Terry. "Also we mustn't look for inventions and progress; it'll be awfully primitive." (Gilman [1915] 1979:8)

The vision of a matriarchal society portrayed in this dialogue focuses on the sexuality of its members, who are perceived as either unthreatening virgins or empty-headed women whose "natural" maternal instincts preclude cooperation among themselves. In any event, matriarchies comprised of celibate females or aggressively protective mothers make societal progress impossible.

The women of the all-female society in *Herland* do not share men's romance of the matriarch. Conventional anthropology, however, subscribes to Terry, Jeff, and Van's views. As an archaic vestige of evolutionism, matriarchy is a discredited idea in anthropology—an idea that subverts the presumed reality of universal male dominance.

Introductory texts and histories of anthropological thought briefly note that matriarchy, which is contrasted with patriarchy as the political rule by men, never existed in any human society. It is commonly asserted in the literature that men have always monopolized important political positions everywhere. Among the Iroquois Indians of North America, for example, principles of matrilineal descent organized society. Genealogical ties and important social relations were reckoned through females; yet the presumption of male supremacy made Iroquois men the dominant social actors.[9]

Matriarchal ideas present both definitional and conceptual problems. Defining matriarchy in political terms assumes relations of sexual inequality; women, rather than men, monopolize power and, presumably, exploit men. Matriarchy, then, is considered the genderized reversal of male dominance. Whether politics necessarily and universally involves sexual hierarchy is not questioned. The possibility that women did, can, or should legitimately exercise political power is ignored in the anthropological literature (Tiffany 1979b, n.d.a , n.d.c).

Matriarchal ideas are also linked to important issues of sexual politics. Categorizing human societies as patriarchal or matriarchal invites distinctions between the powerful and the subordinate and precludes consideration of interdependence and cooperation. Women are the victims in these paradigms. We next consider the dimensions of this victimization in what was considered to be the best of all possible worlds for women in Victorian society.

THE LADY AND THE SAVAGE

The upper-class Victorian woman was refined and indulged. Without protective male overseers, her instability could lead to hysteria—the rebellion of her innate wild nature. At best, the Victorian version of the Wild Woman became the sick woman, dependent and contained. At worst, the Wild Woman as Victorian lady became a petty tyrant (Ehrenreich and English 1978).

Evolutionary theories reinforced the Victorian image of the "perfect lady" as delicate and domestic (Vicinus 1972a; Welter 1966b). Yet, with the exception of a few privileged members of the upper class, the status of perfect lady was difficult, if not impossible, to either achieve or maintain. Middle-class women, most of whom lacked sufficient economic resources to conform to the ideal, comprised a small segment of the population during the Victorian era. Both the image and reality of the perfect lady remained remote and inaccessible.

The significant numbers of working-class women in Victorian Britain presented a disconcerting problem to evolutionary theorists. Some 2 million women were employed in industry and manufacturing by 1911 (which represented a 40 percent increase over 1891), while an additional 1.7 million worked as domestic servants. By 1911, 54 percent of all unmarried women over ten years of age were wage earners (Stearns 1972:109–110). In other words, approximately five million women comprised almost one-third of the total working population in England and Wales by the first decade of this century (Holcombe 1973:213).

Evolutionary theory attempted to reconcile this anomaly by interpreting the perfect lady as a culmination of human progress. The working-class woman, viewed as an archaic survival from an earlier period of underdevelopment, provided stark opposition to the perfect lady (Fee 1974:101; 1976:192). Similarly, the dialectic of civilized and savage that contrasted the West and non-West was reproduced as the savage and civilized within Victorian society. Two versions of the same idea—the perfectly civilized lady and her regressively primitive antithesis, the working-class girl—coexisted in the same society.[10]

Evolutionists encountered difficulties in answering feminist challenges to the patriarchal model of the social order. Other scientific theories, however, marshalled evidence supporting the prevailing paradigm of female nature defined in terms of the submissive wife and mother. The biological principle of inheritance of acquired characteristics, for instance, legitimized the popular idea that psychic differences existed between the sexes. Females were by nature deceptive, intuitive, and irrational (Conway 1972:140–142). Similarly, the physical law of energy conservation was applied to human cell metabolism, in which "the hungry, active cell becomes flagellate sperm, while the quiescent, well-fed one becomes an ovum" (quoted in Conway 1972:144). The dualism of male and female biology resulted, it was argued, in differences of temperament between the sexes. The "katabolic" (active) male who used energy was contrasted with the "anabolic" (passive) female who stored up energy necessary for reproductive functions (Conway 1972:144; Fee 1976:195–200). Biologically determined, male and female temperaments were, therefore, immutable.

These paradigms supported anthropological arguments about the sexual division of labor as a natural and efficient system: men protected and provided for women burdened with pregnancies and childrearing. Few dissented from this view; Margaret Mead did. Stressing the infinite malleability of human temperament, Mead argued the importance of cultural conditioning in shaping individual differences. Her book, *Sex and Temperament in Three Primitive Societies* (Mead 1935), questioned prevailing assumptions of maternal "instincts" and rigid definitions of women as wives and mothers. However, Mead subsequently dismissed her own criticisms of biological reductionism in a later work, *Male and Female* (1949), published during the postwar period in which science and the popular media extolled the ideology of Rosie the Riveter leaving her factory job for her appointed place at home. Spanning half a century, Mead's publications reflect these conflicting ideas about society and gender relations—ideas formulated within the contexts of changing social conditions and political controversies concerning the biological and cultural determinants of human behavior (Tiffany n.d.a, n.d.c).

Recognizing that gender is a cultural construction, rather than a biological given, is important for understanding the Romance of the Wild Woman. Depicted in her varied roles as matriarch or Amazon, as powerless pawn or aggressive castrator, the Wild Woman conveys recurrent themes about female nature expressed in culturally charged idioms of sexuality and submission. Women as mothers, virgins, and whores are, therefore, evocative images in Western thought.

In the remainder of this chapter, we examine the connection between androcentric Victorian notions about women as finely tuned reproductive systems and the Romance of the Wild Woman in anthropological thought.

Body as Woman

Contradiction surrounded nineteenth-century views of Victorian womanhood. In contrast to the carnal and worldly man, the "true" woman possessed greater spirituality, manifested by morally and sexually pure behavior. The ideal of female innocence, however, collided with the proper social duties of being a wife and mother. The true woman's exemplary role as moral guardian over others' behavior coexisted with her responsibility to provide sexual services to her husband.

Woman was a spiritually superior being, but she was also an animal defined and controlled by her reproductive system. The essence of Victorian sexual ideology was neatly summarized by a prominent American (male) gynecologist who wrote in 1847 that woman was "a moral, a sexual, a germiferous, gestative and parturient creature" (quoted in Smith-Rosenberg and Rosenberg 1973:335). Spirituality and the womb expressed the duality of female nature. Biology defined the woman, who imperfectly strived to transcend her physical limitations by acting as society's moral supervisor of her menfolk, children, and home.

Women were simultaneously desired for and denigrated by their bodies. The ambivalence men felt was projected into women's nature. The most compelling images illustrating men's interests in women's bodies concern the female reproductive system. The woman-as-body image reinforced the true Victorian woman as a nervous, hysterical, and sexless entity who submitted to her conjugal duties only out of desire for maternity.

The pure and passionless female is of particular interest for two reasons: she represents a widely held view among many contemporary researchers and the public about Victorian womanhood, and she represents the antithesis of the public nudity and overt eroticism attributed to the Wild Woman of the non-Western world (see chapters 2 and 3).

The relationship between the Victorian ideal of sexual repression and women's actual experiences is ambiguous. Nineteenth-century views of the physiological and sexual aspects of true womanhood were subject to conflicting interpretations. Despite the opinions expressed by some male physicians and numerous marital-advice books current at the time, there is little evidence to support the contention that Victorian women were incapable of expressing sexual feelings. Indeed, members of the medical profession were sharply divided over the issue of female sexuality and the importance of physical gratification for women as part of a healthy marital relationship. More important, we cannot assume that Victorian women inevitably perceived and behaved according to such contradictory ideas about female nature. In fact, it was impossible for women to conform.[11]

Menstrual Paradigms. Dissensus over the nature of Victorian womanhood was further complicated by political considerations. Theories of menstruation current during the nineteenth century illustrate the connection of sex and class with social controversies of the day. Many physicians postulated a link between ovulation and menstruation. Some suggested the moon as a causal factor in triggering menstrual flow. Others argued that menstruation, whatever its origins, was a pathology. Medical experts also disputed the physiological and behavioral effects of menstruation. The "law of monthly periodicity," for example, was believed to influence menstrual or "functional waves," which affected both mind and body (quoted in Bullough and Voght 1973:73). Education and mental exertion, it was argued, would result in irreparable damage to the reproductive system:

> It will have to be considered whether women can scorn delights and live laborious days of intellectual exercise and production, without injury to their functions as the conceivers, mothers, and nurses of

children. For, it would be an ill thing, if it should happen that we got the advantage of a quantity of female intellectual work at the price of a puny, enfeebled, and sickly race. (quoted in Bullough and Voght 1973:73)

The nightmare of bearing and rearing a generation of "enfeebled" progeny was not, however, a concern for all potential mothers.

Class and social background were important considerations in these reproductive paradigms. Thus, the deleterious consequences of menstruation did not uniformly affect the bodies and intellects of all women. Physicians warned upper- and middle-class women against the dangers of mental stimulation and exercise, while asserting that physical labor performed by working-class women during menstruation was not particularly harmful (Bullough and Voght 1973:66–73). The sexual model of promiscuous working-class women, perceived as primitive relics of an earlier evolutionary period, was contrasted with the moral model of upper- and middle-class sexual restraint and civility (Fee 1976:191–195).

Understanding the disparity between the nineteenth-century stereotype of the perfect lady and women's actual experiences is significant for two reasons. First, it shows the power of a dominant ideology, articulated in the semantics of female biology. This reproductive paradigm was accepted by the upper and middle classes of both sexes, including those workers who aspired to higher status. Second, vestiges of the perfect lady idea, particularly the association of women with maternal nurturance and the home, highlight important values in the contemporary West. The ideology of the perfect lady, with its licentious contrast, continues to influence the way in which women's minds and bodies are considered. Although the idea of the "lady" does not accurately depict Western women's lives as housewives, mothers, employees, or lovers, it is, nonetheless, a male-defined indicator of societal values. The ideology of biological constraint shapes and interprets women's realities. It also provides insights into the ways men perceive, evaluate, and explain women as derived, nonmale others.

Weeping Wombs. Menstruation arouses feelings of shame, fear, and resentment among many contemporary Western women who have learned to denigrate the natural functions of their bodies. Recent studies suggest that negative valuations of menstruation persist, especially among women, who have a larger and more diverse repertory of menstrual expressions than men (Culpepper 1979; Ernster 1975). Most female euphemisms for menstruation are disparaging: "falling off the roof," "the curse," "lady troubles," "weeping womb," "bride's barf," and "bloody scourge" (quoted in Ernster 1975:5–7).

Understanding women's experiences and perceptions of their bodies as they pass through the life course is not an important concern in anthropology. Therefore, little comparative material exists on women's bodily processes, including menstruation, pregnancy, parturition, and menopause. The limited literature available on menstruation, which focuses on menstrual prohibitions and ideas of female pollution, conveys a strongly masculine, even misogynous perspective.[12] Cross-cultural studies of menstruation attempted to correlate the presence of menstrual taboos with variables such as penis envy, men's fear of blood, or social patterns that reinforce rigid segregation of the sexes. Men are thought to envy or fear female bodies and their reproductive powers; as a result, men impose restrictions on women during menstruation or childbirth.

The anthropological literature conveys a consistent message about women and their biology: constrained by their reproductive functions, women are unclean and dangerous. Mervyn J. Meggitt's (1964:221) classification of societies in the Highlands of Papua New Guinea illustrates this androcentric point of view:

> ... in Highlands ethnography we must discriminate between at least two kinds of inter-sexual conflict or opposition—the Mae type and

the Kuma type. The one reflects the anxiety of prudes to protect themselves from contamination by women, the other the aggressive determination of lechers to assert their control over recalcitrant women.

According to Meggitt's influential article, women are either contaminating or recalcitrant. Entire social systems, whether in New Guinea or Victorian England, are categorized by male denigration of female biology and the problems Wild Women's bodies pose for men.

Mother as Victim

The Wild Woman may be virginal or provocative, but she can also become a mother. A powerful symbol of both strength and vulnerability, motherhood is associated in the West with dependency and constraint. The feminist literature carries on themes in this persistent mythology. Simone de Beauvoir's book, *The Second Sex* (1952:71), elegantly illustrates the image of the Wild Woman as uncomprehending victim of her own body:

> The woman who gave birth, therefore, did not know the pride of creation; she felt herself the plaything of obscure forces, the painful ordeal of childbirth seemed a useless or even troublesome accident. But in any case giving birth and suckling are not *activities,* they are natural functions; no project is involved; and that is why woman found in them no reason for a lofty affirmation of her existence—she submitted passively to her biological fate. The domestic labors that fell to her lot because they were reconcilable with the cares of maternity imprisoned her in repetition and immanence; they were repeated from day to day in an identical form, which was perpetuated almost without change from century to century; they produced nothing new. (emphasis in original)

A victim of her biological destiny, the Wild Woman does not act, produce, or perform; she merely *is*—passive and unaware.

The powerlessness of motherhood is a common theme in more recent feminist literature as well. Adrienne Rich's statement, (1976:xv) that "for most of what we know as the 'mainstream' of recorded history, motherhood as institution has ghettoized and degraded female potentialities," echoes de Beauvoir's view of women betrayed and victimized by the prisons of their bodies. Similarly, Sara Ruddick (1980:343), in her essay called "Maternal Thinking," writes:

> In most societies however, women are socially powerless in respect to the very reproductive capacities that might make them powerful. The primary bodily experience of mothers is a poignant reminder that to think of maternal power is immediately to recall maternal powerlessness—and conversely.

As these passages illustrate, the politics of biology are integral to the Romance of the Wild Woman. The repetitive, demanding functions of procreation and motherhood are perceived as natural, ancient, immutable, and efficient in supporting the political economy of male dominance. Feminists of other disciplines who use anthropological materials often accept androcentric anthropology, which interprets reproduction as the basis for women's denigration and their appropriation by men. "Women," feminists tell us, "are controlled by lashing us to our bodies" (Rich 1976:xv).

In this chapter we examined metaphors about women. Rehearsed in vocabularies of victimization and sentimentality, the Romance of the Wild Woman elaborates a constellation of ideas, images, and values about women's experiences. The problems that women are thought to pose for men concern relations of gender, sex, and power. Women become silent victims in the processes of explaining and rationalizing the problematic woman in scientific discourse.

In the double bind of oppositions, women are simultaneously desired and denigrated, revered and reviled, approved and appropriated. These invidious contrasts translate women into faceless and silenced nonpersons. Women, the primitive others, are victims of their archaic bodies. Women who menstruate or become mothers are continually reminded of their savage nature. The biological and social categories that define who and what women were, are, and will be include all women—the virginal, the premenstrual, the parturient, the barren, the postmenopausal.

In the next chapter we consider men's encounters with the Wild Woman in other worlds.

2. Encounters with the Wild Woman

We penetrated deeper and deeper into the heart of darkness. It was very quiet there.[1]

Joseph Conrad, 1899

All women are wild, but some are wilder than others. According to this romance, men have tamed some women but not all. In this formulation, culture, identified as male, subdues nature, identified as female. Idealized as docile and sexy pets, civilized women must, however, learn to be "nice" and to suppress their wild nature or be punished. The pornographic picture showing a woman with a horse's bit run through her mouth clearly evokes this metaphor. By comparison, primitive women of the non-Western world are idealized as too naive or childlike in their innocence to understand the necessity of suppression. The nude, overtly sexual native woman, contrasted with the ladylike woman who knows her place, symbolizes a canvas in which male imagination, fantasies, and myth can be safely projected and expressed.[2]

In this chapter we examine the Romance of the Wild Woman as victim and man-eater, with emphasis on the anthropological literature. Translated into a sexualized and private commodity, the Wild Woman is perceived as the servant of men's interests, which are backed by the threat or use of force. Using the language of natural law that defines woman's "place" in nature, the Wild Woman as victim is "good" when she serves the needs of men; conversely, the Wild Woman as man-eater is "bad" when she challenges men or subverts their goals.

Anthropological studies of the Mundurucú Indians of Amazonian Brazil illustrate these invidious contrasts between good and bad women of other worlds. Robert Murphy and Yolanda Murphy interpret social control in Mundurucú society in an explicit vocabulary of male supremacy and physical violence (Murphy 1959, 1960; Murphy and Murphy 1974). Men threaten or resort to force, such as gang rape, to punish women's transgressions. Moreover, Mundurucú women are thought to support male interpretations of the social order and women's secondary "place" in it by punishing each other through "gossip," which can lead to retaliation by the man who feels wronged. Accordingly, "good" women cooperate in their own subjugation by punishing the "bad." In this analysis, the Wild Woman is metamorphosed into an agent of her own denigration.

Taken to its extreme, the "naturalness" of motherhood is shaped by the metaphor of women at the mercy of biological processes—"natural" forces that only men are able to contain. The old adage, "keep them barefoot and pregnant," points to the problem of control that women inevitably present to men in all societies.

The Wild Woman as Victim

Opposition between male and female expresses relations of sexual hierarchy. Thus, the social significance of women is invariably linked to their relationships with men. And, perhaps most important, women, like children, must learn their "place." According to one well-known social anthropologist:

> Almost always, as far as interpersonal relations are concerned, a man claims superior status to his wife. He usually expects her to be

(or at least to appear to be) submissive, humble and obedient, and in many societies he claims the right to beat her if she is not. Of course there are exceptions. (Beattie 1964:133)

Women, like dogs, may have to be beaten into obedience. Women exist in terms of the economic and sexual claims that men rightfully exercise over female labor and bodies. The "exceptions" to this view of human interactions are not discussed.

Themes of male power and female passivity are widespread in the anthropological literature. Indeed, the language of sex and exploitation is crudely explicit in some writings, as in the article by William Divale and Marvin Harris (1976), who described women as ravaged war booty. Misogynistic stereotypes of Australian aboriginal women also illustrate how men are thought to disrespect and mistreat women. C. W. M. Hart and Arnold Pilling's ([1960] 1979:53) ethnography of the Tiwi clearly outlined aboriginal women's place in the social order: "Tiwi wives were as frequently and as brutally beaten by their husbands as wives in any other savage society." Similarly, Meggitt (1962) presented Walbiri women as the classic "brutalized drudge" prototype of Australian aboriginal womanhood. Meggitt's (1962:85–114) chapter on marital relations cited several instances of abuse directed against women.

The implication of such studies is that women's "wrongful" acts encourage male punishment. This interpretation parallels the "rape culture" of American society in which men terrorize women, who are expected to respond as passive, even willing, victims. Both aboriginal and American women thus "cooperate" in their own denigration by inciting men to violence. The Wild Woman—the Australian aboriginal wife/drudge or the battered wife and rape victim in America—deserves whatever men choose to inflict upon her.

Trouble in Paradise

The woman as victim is the implicit subject in anthropologist Derek Freeman's (1983) book, which criticizes Margaret

Mead's Samoan research undertaken between 1925 and 1926. The results of her work were published in *Coming of Age in Samoa* (Mead 1928), the famous book that introduced millions to the delights of sexual awakening in the gentle isles of the South Seas. Freeman's book generated considerable publicity and controversy within academic circles and in the popular media.[3] A brief overview of the history of Mead's fieldwork in the eastern Samoan Islands is necessary in order to understand the background of Freeman's criticism of the research she conducted almost sixty years ago.

On the morning of 31 August 1925, Mead sailed into the magnificent harbor of Pago Pago, American Samoa. Fifty years later she recalled her excitement that day: "Remembering [Robert Lewis] Stevenson's rhapsodies, I was up at dawn to see with my own eyes how this, my first South Sea island, swam up over the horizon and came into view" (Mead 1972:147). Mead embarked on a journey to Polynesia—a journey that would take her into the heart of a Pacific Island society associated with romance and the promise of paradise. She entered this Pacific Eden as a twenty-three-year-old doctoral student in anthropology. Nurtured by the social and political currents of liberalism and feminism, Mead was inspired by the courses she took with her mentor, Professor Franz Boas, the intellectual dynamo of early twentieth-century anthropology at Columbia University.

Mead sought to determine how culture and biology contributed to adolescent behavior in a remote society "untouched" by Western influences. The decision to work in Samoa "proved," Mead (1977:19) later wrote, "to be a most felicitous choice." Mead returned to New York armed with compelling evidence from her Samoan research that learning, rather than genetic endowment, was responsible for the easy transition in Samoa from childhood to adulthood and for the turbulent stresses of adolescence in America.

Mead spent nine months in the Territory of American Samoa: three months on Tutuila, where the port towns of Fagatogo and Pago Pago are located and six months in the village of Ta'ū on the island of the same name in the Manu'a archipelago. Living in the home of Edward Holt, the U.S. Navy's chief pharmacist's mate, along with his wife and children, Mead's research in Ta'ū centered on twenty-five Samoan girls whose ages ranged from fourteen to twenty. Their lives, including their sexual experiences, were the subject of *Coming of Age in Samoa*, the best-selling anthropological book of all time. First published in 1928, *Coming of Age in Samoa*, which has sold millions of copies worldwide, has gone through four editions and has been translated into sixteen languages, including Serbo-Croatian and Urdu. Written for the general reader, *Coming of Age in Samoa* has been widely cited in the popular media and in hundreds of specialized publications from many disciplines.

In the preface to his book, Freeman (1983:xiv) observed: "By the time I left Samoa in November 1943 I knew that I would one day face the responsibility of writing a refutation of Mead's Samoan findings." Freeman has fulfilled his "responsibility." Indeed, his book is a bruising criticism of Mead and her Samoan research. Contending that Mead "was, as a kind of joke, deliberately misled by her adolescent informants" who teased her with lies and "counterfeit tales of casual love under the palm trees," Freeman (1983:240, 290) argued that her conclusions about childrearing, adolescent development, and Samoan social relations, in general, were fundamentally in error. Whereas Mead found ease, cooperation, and easy sex, Freeman found a pathology of conflict, violence, and rape. Instead of a gentle upbringing within the secure warmth of an extended family, Freeman claimed that Samoan children are regularly subjected to harsh punishments by their parents. Instead of nurturance and sharing, Freeman found jealousy, competition, and intense sexual rivalry. Instead of adolescent boys and girls exploring the innocent pleasures of sex, Freeman described a society in which girls and women are terrorized by the omnipresent fear of brutal rape.

Freeman thus presented a dramatically contrary version of

the same society. These differences may be partly explained by the varied contexts of fieldwork experiences, which are unique to each individual researcher. Fieldwork is shaped by the company of one's associates and informants. Freeman (1983:xiii–xv) was quickly inducted into elite politics by having a title conferred upon him early during his research. Avoiding the political arena of status rivalries, Mead (1972:150–154) chose instead to associate with children:

> I concentrated upon the girls of the community. I spent the greater part of my time with them. I studied most closely the households in which adolescent girls lived. I spent more time in the games of children than in the councils of their elders. Speaking their language, eating their food, sitting barefoot and cross-legged upon the pebbly floor, I did my best to minimise the differences between us and to learn to know and understand all the girls of three little villages on the coast of the little island of Taū, in the Manu'a Archipelago. (Mead [1928] 1961:10)

Mead and Freeman each selected a separate domain of study. Researchers who work in ranked societies of Polynesia commonly make such choices, based on considerations of sex, age, and social status.

Yet, the domains of social life that the researcher chooses to emphasize, along with the unique personal experiences of fieldwork, do not sufficiently explain the contrary images of blissful sexuality and savage lust. Differing versions of the Romance of the Wild Woman are also at work in these accounts.

Westerners have always indulged their own visions of what life in the idyllic South Seas should be. Certainly the image of the Pacific Island world as sexually uninhibited but pristine is persistent. In the words of Robert Louis Stevenson ([1900] 1971:2):

> The first experience can never be repeated. The first love, the first sunrise, the first South Sea island, are memories apart and touched a virginity of sense.

Stevenson, affectionately called Tusitala, the "Teller of Tales," lived for many years in Samoa, wrote about it, and died there in 1894. Herman Melville immortalized the Marquesas Islands as a Polynesian playground in his novel *Typee* (1846) and in his narrative of South Seas adventures detailed in *Omoo* (1847).

Mead's *Coming of Age in Samoa* fits into the genre of romantic literature about the search for paradise in other worlds, discussed in this chapter and elsewhere (see chapter 4). In Mead's version, the Wild Woman, supremely self-confident and aware of her powers, actively initiates and controls sexual encounters, not unlike the Amazon of exotic lands (see chapters 1 and 4). Freeman, however, presents a dark vision of the Wild Woman, as powerless victim of savage lust.

The Romance of the Wild Woman as victim is elevated to new heights of woman-hating in Freeman's book. Samoan women are depicted as brutalized sex objects, as well as violent aggressors. Samoan women are irrelevant in Freeman's analysis, except when they are duping Margaret Mead, punishing children, and fighting with other women over men. Samoan women are significant objects of scrutiny to Freeman the anthropologist when they are surreptitiously raped by "sleep-crawlers" or manually "deflowered" by chiefs in public ceremonies. Terrorized by their male assailants who are obsessed by "the cult of virginity" (D. Freeman 1983:234, 250) and fantasies of forcible defloration and rape, Samoan women are transformed into debased Wild Women whose bodies provoke their own oppression (Tiffany 1984, n.d.b, n.d.c).

The Civilized and the Savage

The idea of woman as victim, of course, is not new. Rape and ravishment convey powerful images in Western thought—images that are frequently transferred to exotic worlds. Sexual exploitation is a common theme in the literature of adventurers, missionaries, colonial officers, and novelists. The Wild Women of other worlds are either passively raped or actively seek sexual submission. The continent of Africa, conceptualized in British writings as "the ravished dark woman," expresses the metaphor of sex and conquest (Hammond and Jablow 1970:148). In comparison to the threatening sexuality of African women, Polynesian women invite sexual play, as "white men stood upon the beaches of a dream world, embraced their nymphs, and walked into the golden age" (Daws 1980:2). The idealization of womanhood in the South Seas contrasts sharply with the atavistic perversions of aboriginal women in the tropical New World, who lure outsiders to their destruction while sexually exploiting their own men (Berkhofer 1978:7–12). The eroticism of light-skinned Polynesians and the dark sensuality of African women shift in anthropological and fictional genres to the pragmatic sexuality of Amazonian Indian women, who exchange food for sex or mutely endure men's brutality and sexual abuse.[4] A few Native American women—notably Pocahontas who saved Captain John Smith from death, and Sacagawea who led the Lewis and Clark expedition—escaped such denigration by their transformation into sentimentalized, mythic figures incorporated into American folklore about national origins (Clark and Edmonds 1979; P. Young 1962).

Interestingly, the same Wild Woman was encountered in America, Africa, the South Seas, in fiction, and in anthropology. Despite the variety of geographic locations or literary genres, there is a constancy of perception and interpretation. The Wild Woman conveys Western preoccupation with implicit contrasts of self/other, male/female, civilized/savage, white/black, and Western/non-Western—dualisms articulated in an idiom of sex and power.

The fair lady and the dark woman illustrate the ambivalence of these sexualized contrasts. Characterized by morality and sexual control, the blond lady in fiction opposes the dark-haired schemer. Similarly, the white, civilized lady of temperate climates opposes the dark, primitive woman of the torrid zones. In *Heart of Darkness* Joseph Conrad ([1899] 1971:62) contrasted the eroticism of Kurtz's African mistress, "savage and superb, wild-eyed and magnificent," with his English fiancée—naive, polite, unthreatening, and nonsexual. Herman Melville's ([1846] 1968:204) novel, *Typee: A Peep at Polynesian Life*, vividly described the innocent play of Marquesas Islander women:

> These wilful, care-killing damsels were averse to all useful employment. Like so many spoiled beauties, they ranged through the groves—bathed in the stream—danced—flirted—played all manner of mischievous pranks, and passed their days in one merry round of thoughtless happiness.

Light-skinned women of the South Seas, like the upper-class ladies of England, are mindlessly leisured children. While civilized ladies remain coldly asexual, Polynesian women are unaware of their erotic appeal; and Wild Women of the Dark Continent flaunt it.

The civilized lady represents the sexual restraint of the temperate world, whereas the savage woman embodies the chaos of nature gone mad in the tropics. The Wild Woman of foreign worlds *is* primordial nature, which is hidden within the civilized woman. In contrast to the lady of temperate climes, the Wild Woman of the tropics can never be tamed. Any external trappings of civilization she may acquire comprise a surface veneer to be sloughed off without warning.

Beatrice Grimshaw, a writer of fiction and nonfiction who traveled widely in the Pacific during the late nineteenth and early twentieth centuries, frequently played upon this theme. In a short story set in New Guinea, Grimshaw (1927:7–8) described just such a metamorphosis of civilization regressing to female savagery:

> Sophia, sometimes, looked almost as white as you or I. It seemed to be a matter of feeling. On this day she had drawn down the blind of sulks that is always at the command of the creature cursed with dark blood; she had thickened her lips with pouting, and frowned her brows into projecting ridges that gave her an unpleasant likeness to

the pictures of the Papuan head-hunters on the wall. Yesterday, playing the harmonium at a reunion of coloured church members, she might have passed for a girl of Palermo or Cadiz, had Sicily and Spain been represented in Papua. To-day she was in all essentials, black.

The "dark blood" of savagery flows in the veins of Sophia, a partially civilized "half-caste" who remains the quintessential Wild Woman.

The Wild Woman—pure/perverted, moral/immoral, fair/dark, civilized/savage—suggests compelling metaphors of ambivalence and conflict. Dark heroines and "fallen" women are punished in fiction for their transgressions. Ambitious, powerful women attempt to conceal their "real" selves behind "masks" of ladylike submission as the "blood and thunder tales" of Louisa May Alcott, author of *Little Women*, vividly portray (Stern 1975:xiv; 1976). Such Wild Women are invariably unmasked. The mysterious, perverse, and half-mad women of savage lands in Joseph Conrad's fiction wear no masks. Like the hostile, atavistic tropics, the Wild Women of Conrad's novels victimize civilized men, who are lured to their doom by shedding the restraints associated with an orderly, civil existence. Lurking in an island paradise or a tropical hell, the Wild Woman of Grimshaw's novels is the scheming or naive victimizer of civilized men. The Romance of the Wild Woman as man-eater in fiction is found in anthropological ideas as well.[5]

THE WILD WOMAN AS MAN-EATER

Encounters with other cultures are psychologically turbulent. Anthropologist Bronislaw Malinowski, a pioneer of participant-observation during the early 1900s, recorded feelings of anger and ambivalence in his personal journal, published posthumously by his wife (see Firth 1967; Richards 1968; Stocking 1983; Wax 1972; and M. Young 1979). Malinowski's diary (1967), which was never intended for publication, is an extraordinary human document in which outsiders are privy to emotions that ordinarily remain private.

The perceived realities of exotic other worlds are mental constructs of the researcher. Malinowski was intuitively aware of this in 1914 as his boat neared the Trobriands, the islands that would eventually establish his career in anthropology and that he, in turn, would make famous:

> Joy: I hear the word "Kiriwina" [another name for the Trobriands; also, the main island in the archipelago]. I get ready; little gray, pinkish huts. Photos. *Feeling of ownership: It is I who will describe them or create them.* (Malinowski [1917] 1967:140, emphasis added)

The eager anticipation of mastery quickly turned to disillusionment upon arrival:

> Ashore; comical fences; miserable houses on pilings; . . . The women ran away. . . . I try to talk to them; they run away or tell lies. (Malinowski [1917] 1967:140)

Framed in a sexualized language of desire and denigration, these Pacific isles and their female inhabitants elicit competing feelings of elation, frustration, and rage.

The Nightshade of Pacific Nether Worlds

The theme of the civilized male drawn to his moral and sexual destruction in tropical worlds dominates Malinowski's private writing:

> I felt *joie de vivre tropicale,* something like being drunk on strong wine, at once oppressive and stimulating—broadens horizons and paralyzes you utterly. (Malinowski [1915] 1967:80)

Resisting "subconscious lewdness," "distracting mental lechery," and fantasies of forcible rape, Malinowski sought to reconcile conflicting feelings of impotence and eroticism associated with his "tropical madness" ([1915, 1917] 1967: 112, 113, 68, 69).

Malinowski confused the lure of female sexuality with the fecund, feminized tropics:

> A prostitute or divorcee from *gunika* [inland] *(gunika haine)* [inland woman] attracted my attention—*gagaia ura* [literally, wish sexual intercourse]! (Malinowski [1915] 1967:84)[r]

A few sentences later, Malinowski ([1915] 1967:85) described his surroundings in his diary:

> The smell of the jungle creates a characteristic mood—the subtle, exquisite fragrance of the green *keroro* [tree] flower, lewd swelling of the burgeoning, fertilized vegetation; frangipani—a smell as heavy as incense, with elegant, sharply drawn profile. . . . Rotting trees, occasionally smelling like dirty socks or menstruation, occasionally intoxicating like a barrel of wine "in fermentation."

These words could have been written by Joseph Conrad in his early novel, *An Outcast of the Islands* (1896). Conrad vividly described the tropics as darkly foreboding—like the native woman, Aïssa, who elicits the demons that torment Willems, the white outcast. With the smell of dirty socks and menstruation like that of the rotten jungle, Malinowski conveyed the derogation that white men bring to other worlds.

Malinowski created his own romantic version of Wild Women in the savage South Seas. Images of sexually ripe and wanton women and his lust for them may be found on almost every page of Malinowski's diary. White women provoked him.

> I sat around until 10:30, making up to Mrs. . . . , who is not stupid, though quite uncultured. I fondled her and undressed her in my mind, and I calculated how long it would take me to get her to bed. (Malinowski [1917] 1967:109)

So did Pacific Islander women.

> A pretty, finely built girl walked ahead of me. I watched the muscles of her back, her figure, her legs, and the beauty of the body so hidden to us, whites, fascinated me. Probably even with my own

wife I'll never have the opportunity to observe the play of back muscles for as long as with this little animal. At moments I was sorry I was not a savage and could not possess this pretty girl. (Malinowski [1918] 1967:255)

Like Willems, Malinowski struggled with his own demons attributed to the Wild Women of tropical shores.

Anthropology came of age with fieldwork conducted on the sexual lives of Pacific Islanders. Malinowski's romance of Wild Women in the South Seas upheld Western male privileges in an explicit vocabulary of lust and revulsion—vocabulary submerged in his academic writings intended for publication. Malinowski subsequently wrote about kinship and marriage among the Trobriand Islanders in several important books, including one with the provocative title *The Sexual Life of Savages in North-Western Melanesia*, published in 1929—one year after Mead's *Coming of Age in Samoa*. A brief sentence written in his diary in 1918 reveals a darker side of Malinowski's interest in the sex lives of the islanders: "Talked with the *niggers* about 'the positions' during sexual intercourse" ([1918] 1967:260, emphasis in original).

Feminist historian Mary Ritter Beard ([1942] 1977: 219-220), a contemporary of Malinowski, criticized his functionalist and ahistorical approach to the study of non-Western societies. Beard ([1942] 1977:219) charged Malinowski with "extremely masculine conceptual thinking," a critique unrecorded in the literature concerning Malinowski's contributions to anthropological thought (see also Lane 1977). Malinowski's voluminous writings on the Trobriand Islands are notable for the invisibility of women. Indeed, the first work to examine gender relations in the Trobriands—a subject ignored by the male anthropologists who came after Malinowski—was published almost sixty years after Malinowski's fieldwork expeditions between 1914 and 1920 (see Weiner 1976).

The Wild Woman in Anthropology

Anthropological knowledge about the Wild Woman is built on value-loaded meanings of sex and gender. These selective meanings emphasize what researchers perceive they know, or ought to know, about women in other societies. The anthropologist simultaneously plays the roles of "self" and "outsider" while conducting fieldwork, which entails observing and recording the actions of "others" who are also "insiders," or informants (see chapter 1). The Romance of the Wild Woman interprets what indigenous others are thought to perceive as their own social and existential realities. Women, however, do not speak for themselves in these romanticized accounts.

Outsiders' knowledge obtained about women is multilayered. Statements about women are diffused through the anthropologist's initial prism, which consists of unexamined assumptions about gender relations cast in a language of male power. This initial prism is subsequently diffused through another lens—that of the male informant, who interprets women's behavior on two different levels of meaning: what the informant thinks he and other men in that society understand about women, and what the informant attributes to the researcher's understandings and interests.

Women are likely to be excluded from this discourse for several reasons. First, male informants may discount or disregard women's views. Second, the anthropologist rarely talks with women, or he avoids them. Third, the anthropologist asks questions of women and observes them in preselected domains, such as housekeeping and childcare, where it is assumed that women are active and visible. Finally, the anthropologist primarily collects and distills these refracted interpretations from men and diffuses these through the prism of scientific description and explanation. At this level, anthropological knowledge is published, applied to the research, teaching, and writing of professionals in anthropology and other disciplines, and perhaps disseminated (if it is a controversial topic) into the popular media.[7]

Women, then, are excluded from participation in anthropological inquiry at two levels. First, women who conduct research and interpret anthropological knowledge are socialized to accept the existing framework of professional values of universities and professional organizations—institutions controlled by men. Silenced women of the society under study constitute a second critical level of analysis. Women of other worlds are rendered inarticulate by dominant modes of inquiry, which originate with the anthropologist-outsider who presumes that important knowledge is acquired and controlled by men. Encompassed within the domains of men's relationships and understandings, women at both levels of inquiry—as researchers and as subjects of observation—are bereft of their own voices.

The Romance of the Wild Woman as victim articulates the semantics of power and coercion that runs through anthropology and literature. A "battle-of-the-sexes" view of human relations, in which women are cast as victimizers of men or their victims, is a powerful myth.

The reader of anthropological studies should, therefore, ask why the following quotations from informants were selected for publication instead of others: A Mundurucú man claims, "We tame our women with the banana" (quoted in Murphy [1959] 1973:220); Sharanahua women of Amazonian Peru say, "there's no meat, let's eat penises," if men come back from the hunt empty-handed (quoted in Siskind 1973b:105). Kuma men of Highland New Guinea assert, "'women are nothing,' and women retaliate, 'men are no good'" (quoted in Meggitt 1964:205). The theme of sexual antagonism, articulated in a vocabulary of castrating females, phallic power, and institutionalized hostility between men and women is commonplace in anthropological writings, particularly about indigenous peoples of South America and Highland New Guinea. The stridently sexual "man-eater" reinforces anthropologists' ambivalent perceptions of the Wild Woman as politically impotent but sexually threatening.

The Romance of the Wild Woman also reveals what is *not*

said about her. When reading about the Wild Woman in anthropology, we must seek for covert agendas of meaning. What selective processes, for example, led to Freeman's (1983:250) conclusion that in Samoa "the cult of female virginity is probably carried to a greater extreme than in any other culture known to anthropology"? The answer lies in the Romance of the Wild Woman inhabiting a South Seas paradise.

3. The Primitive Woman

Anthropology is but a latter-day version of the descent into hell, into a strange and bizarre underworld, in which the hero—disguised as The Investigator—walks untouched among the shades because he carries in his hand the magic sword of Science.[1]

Eric R. Wolf, 1964

Exotic nether worlds provide the backdrop against which the outsider scrutinizes and evaluates the Wild Woman. In this chapter we survey anthropological versions of the Wild Woman as primitive in three prominent ethnographies: the Nuer of Africa, the Tiwi of Australia, and the Yanomama of South America. These particular societies were chosen for two reasons.

Research on these peoples significantly influenced anthropological ideas about gender and sex. E. E. Evans-Pritchard's works on the Nuer, which remain essential reading for graduate students, contributed to the structural-functional school of anthropological theory and influenced the work of generations of subsequent students. Ethnographies of the Tiwi and Yanomama, written as introductions to the study of non-Western peoples and published in inexpensive editions, are widely used in undergraduate university courses in anthropology. In sum, studies of the Nuer, Tiwi, and Yanomama have considerable impact on professional students of anthropology and on undergraduates, who are taught about the human condition by having the primitive serve as the contrast to their own way of life.

The second reason for selecting these ethnographies is more complex. We are confronted in these studies with archetypes of the savage that coincided with the colonial presence. Exploitation and intimidation describe relations between women and men. The primitive Wild Woman, voiceless and victimized in these accounts, reinforces mythic structures of desire and denigration recurrent in anthropological literature about other worlds. The myth of the savage male and the not-so-innocent female is recreated and embellished in anthropological discourse about indigenous others. The Wild Woman thus continues to intrigue the outsider-observer.

THE NUER: WOMEN'S PLACE IN AN AFRICAN SOCIETY

In 1930 the Nuer of southern Sudan comprised some two hundred thousand people who practiced a mixed economy of cattle herding supplemented with millet and maize cultivation. E. E. Evans-Pritchard's published works on the Nuer, based on brief periods of research during the 1930s, are classics in British social anthropology. His studies provided an important framework for interpreting social processes firmly grounded in observation and detailed description. Evaluating Evans-Pritchard's contributions to the development of anthropological theory is not attempted here.[2] Rather, we concentrate on Evans-Pritchard's paradigm of Nuer society and its implications for women. Our discussion of the Nuer and the Wild Woman considers three related problems: descent as a principle of social structure, bridewealth and the exchange of women, and social order and the Wild Woman.

The Problem of the Wild Woman

Evans-Pritchard's model of Nuer society is built upon specific assumptions about the organization of patrilineal (agnatic) descent and women's peripheral roles in such systems.[3] The Nuer form of patriliny is "a highly segmented genealogical structure" consisting of "maximal" and "minimal" lineages grouped in agnatic clans (Evans-Pritchard 1940a:192).[4] Accordingly, Nuer women are socially important as mothers, sisters, and wives of men; women are defined in terms of their sexuality and exchange value for men, and women are dominated by men.

In Evans-Pritchard's view, Nuer lineages involve men in political relations of opposition and cohesion, fission and fusion. By emphasizing male-controlled lineages as institutions of social order, it is possible, using Evans-Pritchard's model of the Nuer, to conceptualize an entire society in terms of patrilineal descent and male dominance. Women in this paradigm assume sexual value. As potential or actual mothers who bear children for men's lineages, women acquire functional importance as breeders and socializers of the young, not unlike the Victorian ideal of true womanhood.

Evans-Pritchard's androcentrism is combined with his structural-functional approach to relations of kinship and descent as a legal problem. The transmission of political rights over women, children, and property among men is a primary concern in this paradigm, which does not accord women legal or political entitlements. Daughters are defined as legal minors of their fathers, and upon marriage husbands acquire guardianship over their wives. Nuer women, therefore, are categorized as the chattel of men.

The Nuer are considered a classic example in the anthropological literature of how a patrilineal system works. Read by generations of undergraduate and graduate students, Evans-Pritchard's publications on the Nuer interpret and confirm human reality as a male world. By emphasizing male control of women, patrilineal descent emerges as the overriding principle of social organization that explains how Nuer society operates (Evans-Pritchard 1973a:1). Thus, observed behaviors that do *not* fit this now-archetypal model create difficulties for the anthropologist. Such problems led Evans-Pritchard (1951:28) to conclude:

> It would seem it may be partly just because the agnatic principle is unchallenged in Nuer society that the tracing of descent through women is so prominent and matrilocality so prevalent. However much the actual configurations of kinship clusters may vary and change, the lineage structure is invariable and stable.

Evans-Pritchard's own data show that Nuer lineages are not "invariable." Indeed, many people trace descent through females, rather than males as required by the patrilineal rule. Evans-Pritchard tried to explain this anomaly by arguing that the principle of patrilineal descent is "unchallenged" dogma and, therefore, unaffected by people's behavior. By upholding the fiction of patrilineal descent, premised on reckoning genealogical connections exclusively through males and the legal dominance of men, Evans-Pritchard dismissed Nuer women as muted and shadowy participants in the structure of their own society.

Kinship relations among Nuer women—as sisters, mothers, daughters, or co-wives—are briefly discussed in a few sentences, in contrast to the extended treatment of male kin (Evans-Pritchard 1951:152–180; see also Gough 1971:113–115). Described as helpmates to their male relatives or husbands, women are then dismissed. In discussing domestic organization and parent-child relations, Evans-Pritchard (1951:145) wrote:

> Only the position of sons is considered. Daughters will not remain with either their genitor [biological father] or the kinsmen of their pater [social father], but will become members of their hubands' households. Control over their persons is therefore not disputed, and division of their bridewealth is so well defined by custom that it is a matter of minor importance where they are brought up.[5]

Daughters are mentioned in the context of male control, but Evans-Pritchard considered sons crucial for understanding domestic organization. As this passage suggests, Nuer women are neither individuals nor decision makers. Rights to their persons are exercised by men, and male consensus concerning men's rights to transfer women reinforce established customary rules that mechanically shift women from their fathers' to their husbands' jurisdiction.

Evans-Pritchard's conclusions, however, are disputed by his own data, which suggest a more complex view of women than he allowed in his model. Nuer women may enter a variety of marital, extramarital, or consensual unions with men. Moreover, some women choose to remain single instead of marrying. Other enterprising women, particularly members of aristocratic lineages, become "men" (discussed below) by assuming the rights and obligations associated with being a husband and a father in Nuer society (Evans-Pritchard 1951:104–123). Alice Singer's (1973:86) reassessment of Evans-Pritchard's work contends that Nuer wives and mothers are neither political subordinates nor passive chattel:

> Both a woman and her children have so much freedom of choice and mobility that they may exercise their own "rights" even to the detriment of their husbands, fathers, or brothers. . . . Many women are not under any man's authority. They may rear families without consenting to marriage, own cattle, have legal personalities, take their small children with them when they change residence, and sometimes control households.

Evans-Pritchard's model of Nuer social structure reflects an unquestioned assumption about the subordinate roles of women. It disallows consideration of women's options and strategies for modifying the rules of social structure by their decisions and actions.

Bridewealth and the Exchange of Women

The use of commercial and legal vocabulary in reference to women is widespread in the anthropological literature. Depicted as "liquid asset[s]" (quoted in Service 1971:35) and as "a kind of property" (Beattie 1964:194), women are "the most precious of all currencies" (Lewis 1976:234). Evans-Pritchard (1951:98) described Nuer bridewealth (brideprice) in economic terms as "an exchange of cattle for a wife." A woman's worth is equivalent to a determined number of cattle. In addition to describing women as purchaseable commodities through bridewealth transfers, women's roles as wives are cast in a legalistic terminology that defines and emphasizes men's conjugal rights. A. R. Radcliffe-Brown ([1935] 1952:32–33), an advocate of structural-functionalism in anthropology, distinguished two types of claims over persons, both of which emphasize the conjugal rights of husbands over wives. Rights *in uxorem* refer to a husband's sexual and domestic claims over his wife; rights *in genetricem* refer to a husband's claims to any children his wife may bear. In either case, these terms ignore the marital and parental rights of women.[6]

This androcentric perspective is part of a theoretical tradition that views marriage as the exchange of women. According to Claude Lévi-Strauss (1969:480–481), a major proponent of this approach, women are valuables that men use to initiate or solidify relationships with each other. Anthropologists consider women as commodities that men manipulate in order to enhance their political and economic interests. Note, for instance, how Evans-Pritchard (1951:122) depersonalized women in his account of bridewealth transactions:

> It is the fertility of the womb which a lineage receives by payment of bridewealth. All children born of that womb belong to the lineage; they are all agnates.

Women are no longer persons, let alone sisters, daughters, or wives; rather, they are "wombs." The Wild Woman, bereft of mind and volition, is simply a uterus.

Evans-Pritchard (1951:104–123) detailed various unions other than "normal matrimony" in which Nuer husbands are said to exercise conjugal rights over women by making cattle payments to their wives' lineages. Legal unions include polygyny (marriage of one man to two or more women simultaneously), as well as leviratic and ghost marriages, which recognize men's conjugal rights after their deaths. In addition, some Nuer women marry other women and assume the role of husbands (Evans-Pritchard 1951:108–109).[7] Widows may take male lovers, while other women may choose to remain unattached (Evans-Pritchard 1951:113–120).

The frequency with which these varied types of same- and opposite-sex unions occur in Nuer society is significant. According to one analysis of Evans-Pritchard's figures, "just under half the women of childbearing age are under the legal guardianship of no man" (Gough 1971:109). These data suggest, then, that the Nuer social structure and women's roles are more complex than the rules governing husbands' conjugal rights and the exchange of "wombs" among men imply.

Social Order and Women's "Station"

Politics presented a problem in Evans-Pritchard's paradigm of Nuer social structure. The Nuer have neither government nor law; they exist in a system of "ordered anarchy" characterized by the absence of rulers, including formal legislative, executive, and judicial institutions (Evans-Pritchard 1940a:5–6; 1940b:293, 296). Evans-Pritchard's (1940a: 7–15, 66–69) concern with social order was especially compelling, given the contexts of a brutal pacification by the British and a destructive cattle disease afflicting the Nuer at the time of his research. The "intractable" nature of the Nuer "country and character" encouraged the formulation of metarules imposed on the chaotic, recalcitrant Nuer social life (Evans-Pritchard 1940a:9; 1973b:19).

The problem of Nuer social order also involves internal political problems posed by Nuer women who violate the rules of their society. Nuer women, Evans-Pritchard (1951:134) wrote, are "well content with their station." Nonetheless, as Evans-Pritchard noted in several places (1947; 1951:57, 95, 104, 133–134), women neither meekly accept male coercion, "bullying," and physical abuse, nor the decisions of their husbands, fathers, or male guardians. Like their ecology and society, Nuer women seem intractable. The wildness of Nuer women is commonly displayed by their stubborn insistence on being other than quiescent objects exchanged for cattle. In Evans-Pritchard's formulation, Nuer women represent chaos and disorder in a system defined and controlled by the imposition of male interests.

In a lecture on the "position of women" delivered about twenty years after his Nuer research, Evans-Pritchard (1965:45) contrasted "modern civilized woman and her savage sister." His depiction of the Wild Woman disputed much of his own fieldwork among the Nuer. According to Evans-Pritchard (1965:45), the primitive woman has no choice but to marry, and as a result of her full-time responsibilities as wife and mother, she "is therefore seldom able to take much part in public life." Furthermore, the primitive woman accepts her station.

> She does not regard herself as being at a disadvantage, and she does not envy her menfolk what we describe as their privileges. She does not desire, in this respect, things to be other than they are; and it would greatly puzzle her if she knew that in our society many women are unmarried and childless. (Evans-Pritchard 1965:45)

These remarks are intriguing, since Nuer women do not necessarily accept male definitions of their "place." Moreover, the statement that marriage is the only option available to primitive women refutes Evans-Pritchard's observation that Nuer women enter casual liaisons, marry other women, or choose to remain single. Referring to never-married Nuer women as "unmarried concubines," Evans-Pritchard (1951:118) wrote that these women readily accepted and rejected lovers as they moved from village to village. Such women were not anomalies. Evans-Pritchard (1951:118) found unmarried women, many of whom were also mothers, in every village where he asked about them. Moreover, he described single women as persons "of strong character who valued their independence and did not desire matrimony" (Evans-Pritchard 1951:118).

Primitive women, according to Evans-Pritchard, are ideally parturient, domestic, and obedient—the classic Victorian definition of the true woman transferred to the Nilotic savanna. Thus, the anthropological literature also reminds us that the Wild Woman is a universal to be found in the historical past and in present-day cultural diversity.

THE AUSTRALIAN TIWI: GAMES SAVAGES PLAY

Tiwi women, like the Nuer, are also recalcitrant. In addition, the Tiwi Wild Woman poses special kinds of problems for the men who have observed her. Generations of students and professionals have read and been influenced by almost a century of anthropological research on Australian aborigines. Conducted primarily by male anthropologists, these studies relied primarily on aboriginal men for information about women. Emphasis on male supremacy added an additional prism of sex to anthropological knowledge of the Wild Woman in aboriginal societies undergoing drastic change in a colonial setting.

Anthropologists' studies of Australian aborigines seemed to confirm what researchers expected to find: men are important, women are insignificant and oppressed. Phyllis Kaberry's classic work, *Aboriginal Woman: Sacred and Profane* (1939), ignored by anthropologists for many years after its publication, contradicted "the widespread idea that Aboriginal women are mere drudges, passing a life of monotony and being shamefully ill-treated by their husbands" (Elkin 1939:xxii). Kaberry's study demonstrated that aboriginal women's productive contributions are crucial for group survival; moreover, women are important participants in the political and religious institutions of their societies.[8]

However, denigrating stereotypes of aboriginal women continue in more recent literature. Tiwi women and girls, for example, are described in one anthropological study as the "chattels," "currency," and "political capital" of men. Older women are referred to as "old crones" and "toothless old hag[s]," in comparison to neutral references to "older men" and "senior men" (Hart and Pilling [1960] 1979:14, 35, 52–53, 75, 80). This pejorative language illustrates how researchers "project on the aboriginal women the contempt and disrespect to which the older woman is subject in Western society" (Rohrlich-Leavitt 1976:199). To be wild and female is sufficient liability, but to be old and female elicits revulsion. As anthropologist Jules Henry (1963:449) observed, "the usual picture of the aged primitive woman is that, half naked and unkempt she does not conceal from view her spent body."

Anthropological studies of the Tiwi are of special interest to students of aboriginal social systems because a number of researchers who have worked in the same society interpret gender relations in different ways. Hart and Pilling's ([1960] 1979) ethnography, which is widely used in undergraduate anthropology courses, presented Tiwi men as gamesters and women as dependent drudges. However, Jane Goodale's book, *Tiwi Wives* (1971), described a more complex world of opposite- and same-sex relationships. Female experiences and perceptions are an important focus of Goodale's work, which depicted women as vital and productive social actors.[9] These conflicting interpretations demand further inquiry.

Mothers and Wives in Polygynous Marriages

The Tiwi, who are no strangers to external contact and Western influence, live on Melville and Bathurst Islands, located about twenty-five miles off the north coast of Australia. The first mission station was established on Bathurst at the turn of the century. By the mid-1950s, most Tiwi were attached to one of several missions on the islands and were dependent on Western goods, particularly tobacco and trade store foodstuffs.

Tiwi men prefer the polygynous form of marriage. Polygyny in Tiwi society results in withdrawing young women from the marriageable population who would otherwise be available as wives to men of similar ages. As a consequence, younger males (those under thirty-five) must seek widows as wives, some of whom are beyond childbearing age. Senior women are nonetheless important to a man's survival, since they are knowledgeable about food resources and teach productive skills to less experienced co-wives.

The significance of the Tiwi system of marriage from a woman's perspective is that she can expect to marry several times during her lifetime. A woman's first husband is usually considerably older (the average age difference between spouses is about nineteen years), since she may have been promised before puberty to a man already in his thirties or forties. A woman, therefore, expects to outlive a succession of husbands. And, as she matures, her decisions in selecting a future spouse, including husbands for her daughters and granddaughters, become politically significant (Goodale 1962).

According to Hart and Pilling [(1960] 1979:33), "What held the [domestic] unit together was the central position and dominance of the father or husband, and hence the life of a household was only as long as his lifetime." Closer examination of Hart and Pilling's data suggests another interpretation. Goodale (1971:74) argued that related women provide group continuity, since sisters frequently marry the same man as they achieve sexual maturity. Female sibling (sister-sister) ties are reinforced, since sisters are likely to "move as a unit of co-wives into the domestic group of their successive and common husbands" (Goodale 1971:74). In other words, sisters grow up together, often marry the same man, and move as a unit to their new husband's camp. Successive marriages do not break up these female relationships; rather, sisters continue to provide mutual assistance, regardless of who their common husband happens to be at the time.

Women and Politics in the Australian Outback

"The Sons of Turimpi," an article published by Hart in 1954, illustrates the failure to recognize the importance of Tiwi mothers in the lives of children of both sexes. By focusing on men, Hart overlooked significant patterns of gender relations that emerge in his own data. Depicted as a passive backdrop to men's activities, the Wild Woman emerges as a powerful figure in Tiwi society, despite Hart's title.

Hart's essay described five men, who are full and half-brothers. Three of these brothers are the sons of Turimpi, an important political figure, and his wife, Bongdadu. After the death of Turimpi, which occurred around the turn of the century, Bongdadu remarried and bore two more sons (Hart 1954:244). "The Sons of Bongdadu" is a more appropriate title for Hart's article for one simple reason: These five men consider themselves brothers because they share a mother. Bongdadu, not Turimpi, provided continuity in the lives of her five sons. Indeed, Turimpi died while his own three sons were children. The central figure, then, in the lives of Tiwi men and women is their mother. The disparity in ages between spouses means that fathers are unlikely to live long enough to see all their children grow into adulthood. This elementary demographic fact is important for understanding the genealogical and political significance of Tiwi women.

Hart and Pilling ([1960] 1979:132–133) recognized that genealogies are keys to understanding the dynamics of Tiwi social organization. Fascinated with male intrigues, Hart and Pilling erred by dismissing a critical point in their own data. Senior women memorize, disseminate, and, therefore, control, genealogical information. The implications of women having such knowledge to give or withhold were ignored.

Like the Nuer, Tiwi women are depicted as brutalized commodities used to further the cynical and occasionally ridiculous interests of men. The function of Tiwi women is to serve as men's dependent pawns; women are "political capital available for investment in gaining the goodwill of other men"; they are "the main currency of the influence struggle, the main 'trumps' in the endless bridge game [of men]" (Hart and Pilling [1960] 1979:52). Politics, for Hart and Pilling, is gamesmanship. Tiwi men engage in ritualized displays of hostility toward other men, such as spear fights between cuckolded husbands and their wives' lovers. However, the implicit message behind such incidents is that women are responsible when men fight each other. The "payoff" for men's political games is, from Hart and Pilling's perspective, power and prestige articulated through the medium of women.

Reducing women to objects—chattel, capital, trumps, or currency—divests women of volition and voices to speak for themselves. The hidden message of the female-as-chattel perspective in both the Tiwi and Nuer studies is that women have neither options nor opinions. This view is consistent with conventional anthropological assumptions that women are political pawns whose lives and aspirations are defined by men's interests.

Comparison of the Tiwi literature, like the controversy over Samoa (discussed in chapter 2), illustrates how assumptions about sex and gender can result in differing emphases and conclusions (Tiffany 1984). Senior Tiwi women are keepers of genealogical knowledge, a source of political power and authority in this kinship-based society. Thus, Tiwi wives and mothers are not passive onlookers of men's affairs; they are active participants in the political process, rather than mere collaborators with or subverters of male decisions. Studies of the Tiwi also pose critical questions about the anthropological enterprise and the consequences of perceiving the primitive Wild Woman, like the true Victorian woman, through the prism of sex.

Whose perceptions of the Wild Woman are emphasized or disregarded in anthropological inquiry, and why? Let us consider this question as we shift from the Tiwi male as savage gamester to the Yanomama male as brutal aggressor.

RAGE AND RAPE AMONG THE AMAZONIAN YANOMAMA

The Yanomama Indians, who number approximately twelve thousand, live in the tropical forests of southeastern Venezuela and northwestern Brazil. The Yanomama are the best-known example in anthropology of an indigenous Indian society in the Amazon region because of Napoleon Chagnon's (1968b, 1977, 1983) ethnography, the most popular book in a series of case studies intended for college students.

The Yanomama, whom Chagnon called the "fierce people," are depicted as violent and misogynous. The savage male in Amazonia, living in a "counterfeit paradise" of deceptively lush vegetation, engages in incessant warfare against enemies, ritualized hostility with men, and the physical abuse of women. The savage is stripped of his nobility, as Chagnon's (1983:10) description of his initial encounter with Yanomama men illustrates:

> I looked up and gasped when I saw a dozen burly, naked, sweaty, hideous men staring at us down the shafts of their drawn arrows! Immense wads of green tobacco were stuck between their lower teeth and lips making them look even more hideous, and strands of dark-green slime dripped or hung from their nostrils—strands so long that they clung to their pectoral muscles or drizzled down their chins.

As Chagnon (1977:6) noted, "So much for my discovery that primitive man is not the picture of nobility and sanitation I had conceived him to be." Transformed into the debased wild man, the ignoble savage earns our contempt. Chagnon reminds us that there is no paradise in the Amazonian New World, there is only deception and violence.

Chagnon was introduced to a Yanomama village by the missionary who had lived there for five years. This village was home base for the missionary, who had sustained contact with the Yanomama since the 1950s. Chagnon set up camp in the missionary's empty mud hut during his absence (Chagnon 1983:9–12). Perhaps the Indians' give-me ploys, described by Chagnon (1983:15) as "incessant, passioned, and often aggressive demands," can be attributed to the context of such missionary efforts.

The flow of Western trade goods into Yanomama hands

through missionary endeavors is, in Chagnon's (1983:61) words, "nothing short of incredible." One missionary Chagnon knew had distributed, during a fourteen-year period, more than three thousand steel machetes to the 130 members of his village (Chagnon 1983:61). Nevertheless, Chagnon (1983:4–41) persists in interpreting Yanomama demands for foreign goods as a manifestation of greed by primitive men living in a Hobbesian version of society hitherto uncontacted by civilization.

Victims and Victimizers in the Tropics

Three images of the Wild Woman as primitive are conveyed in Chagnon's book and in anthropologist Marvin Harris's (1974) interpretation of the Yanomama: women are brutalized, women are the political currency of men, and women cooperate in their own debasement.

Chagnon's ethnography contains many references to male abuse of women (1977:15, 82–84, 95, 123; 1983:27, 111–114, 123, 175–176). Men gang rape women captured from other villages. Husbands beat their wives with fists or firewood, slash them with machetes or axes, shoot them with barbed arrows in a "nonvital area, such as the buttocks or leg," burn them with glowing sticks, rip their ear lobes, cut off their ears, and occasionally murder them. According to Chagnon (1977:83), "It is considered good to beat a wife every once in a while just to show your concern for her." In his chapter entitled "The Savage Male," Harris (1974:88) catalogued male violence against women: "All Yanomamo men physically abuse their wives. Kind husbands merely bruise and mutilate them; the fierce ones wound and kill." Other anthropologists who have worked with the Yanomama—notably Jacques Lizot (1976a, 1977), Alcida Ramos (1979), and Judith Shapiro (1976)—criticized the "hyperfierce image" of these people (quoted in Chagnon 1977:163). Interestingly, in the second and third editions of his ethnography, Chagnon (1977:162–164; 1983:213–214) attempted, in a limited way, to redress the widely held view of Yanomama men as warlike aggressors who continually brutalize women—a view that he himself promoted.[10]

The Wild Woman as political currency is a key metaphor in the anthropology of other worlds. In Chagnon's analysis, Yanomama men exchange rights over women and, if necessary, take them by force from men who refuse to cede them. The "politics of brinksmanship," based on bluff, threat, coercion, chicanery, violence, and even murder, encompasses women as pawns of intervillage alliances or feuds (Chagnon 1977:68–70, 97–102). According to this interpretation, the ideology of male dominance is maintained by brutal displays of force. Women, by contrast, are oppressed, serving as degraded chattel and prizes of war. In Chagnon's political model, Wild Women exist only in terms of male-defined interests and constraints. Among the Yanomama, the Wild Woman has neither social presence nor voice. She is dehumanized.

In contrast to her image as brutalized booty, the Yanomama Wild Woman is also an agent of discord among men. Accordingly, the Wild Woman is said to contribute to her own victimization. Like the American rape victim considered responsible for unleashing the sexual urges of her male assailant by her enticing behavior, Yanomama women cause men, in Chagnon's analysis, to club and raid each other. Accordingly, Yanomama and American women provoke their own oppression. They are the prizes of men's contests in which rape is a reward for aggression.

Darwinian processes of sexual selection, whereby the fiercest males monopolize the greatest number of women and therefore sire more children than less aggressive men, are used to explain the relationship between power and reproduction in Yanomama society (Chagnon 1968a, 1975; Chagnon et al. 1970; Chagnon and Irons 1979; M. Harris 1974:103–105). In this "rape culture" interpretation of Yanomama society, sexual violence against women is considered a natural act associated with being male. Rape is treated as an important social mechanism whereby men acquire power and prestige over women, as well as over other men who control women.

Women's reproductive biology is not, however, viewed in the same "adaptive" framework as rape and sexual selection. Menstruation, a regular reminder of the Wild Woman's atavistic body, reveals the ideological symmetry of sexual desire and denigration that defines the Wild Woman as victim in anthropology. Consider the following ways in which three anthropologists convey the Romance of the Wild Woman in their discussions of menstrual seclusion. Two (Chagnon and Lizot) conducted research among the Yanomama, while a third (Harris) interpreted Chagnon's material.

Lizot (1976a:108) described Remaema, an initiate who had just completed her menstrual seclusion:

> There is magnificent Remaema; her body is covered with adornments and the heady perfume of flowers and plants; she conveys a provocative and charming sensuality; her face shows a quiet joy. . . .
> Remaema re-enters the communal house [*shabono*]; she walks around the central plaza in a quiet and assured step, she goes to the place of her parents. . . . The high voices of women sing; she [Remaema] is no longer an immature *(ruwë)* girl, she is strong *(tat^{h}e)* now, her menstrual blood proves it. [our translation]

Compare this passage with Chagnon's (1983:115) description of seclusion at first menses:

> Yąnomamö girls are confined to their houses and hidden behind a screen of leaves. . . . The Yąnomamö word for menstruation translates literally as "squatting" *(roo)*, and that fairly accurately describes what pubescent females (and adult women) do during menstruation. Yąnomamö women do not use the equivalents of tampons or sanitary napkins. They simply remain inactive during menstruation, squatting on their haunches and allowing the menstrual blood to drip on the ground.

Finally, consider Harris's (1974:90) account of Chagnon's interpretation of female initiation:

> Like other male-dominated cultures, the Yanomamo think menstrual

blood is evil and dangerous. When a girl has her first menses they lock her up inside a specially constructed bamboo cage and force her to go without food. Thereafter, she must isolate herself at every menstrual period and remain squatting alone in the shadow of the house.

Each writer communicates differing images and meanings of female bodies and biological processes.

Initiation to womanhood is a positive experience for Yanomama girls, according to Lizot's romanticized description of the Wild Woman as object of desire. Chagnon acknowledged the social significance of her first menstruation, but he stressed the constraints imposed on women, who are passive victims of their biological processes. Thus, Yanomama women are portrayed as doing little else but "squatting" during their monthly cycles. Harris provided a misogynous interpretation of menstruation. For Harris, the "screen of leaves" in Chagnon's account is transformed into a "bamboo cage" for the initiate. Both sexes, according to Harris, are contemptuous and fearful of women's bodies. But Remaema, described by Lizot, seems to feel no such loathing.

Infanticide and Warfare. Male power and the threat of female sexuality are linked to explanations of why an imbalanced sex ratio favoring males occurs in some Yanomama communities. Chagnon (1968:139) connected the disparity of numbers between the sexes to the practice of female infanticide, particularly in regions where raiding and warfare are intense. According to Chagnon, men desire sons, especially as the firstborn; they consider daughters less "useful," and they are eventually transferred to other men upon marriage:

> Male babies are preferred because they will grow up to be warriors and hunters. Most men make known their wishes to have a son—even to the point of insinuating that the wife ought to deliver a male or suffer the consequences. This is always done in a subtle way, usually by displaying signs of anger or resentment at the thought of having a daughter that constantly eats without being potentially an

economic asset or guardian of the village. Many women will kill a female baby just to avoid disappointing their husbands. (Chagnon 1977:75)

The resulting scarcity of females escalates feuding and warfare as men attempt to abduct women or coerce men from less powerful villages into giving away their women.

Lizot (1977:501–505), however, questioned the relationship between female infanticide and warfare. He claimed that infanticide of either sex is infrequent, comprising less than 2 percent of births. There is no compelling evidence, according to Lizot, to suggest that sons are preferred to daughters.

Chagnon (1977:74) acknowledged that male infanticide also occurred. Indeed, infanticide of either sex is likely to take place in case of physical deformity or twin births. The close arrival of a new infant, which would jeopardize the health of a child still nursing, may also occasion infanticide (Chagnon 1977:74–75; Lizot 1977:504). Lizot further suggested that a sex ratio favoring males did not necessarily mean female babies were killed at higher rates. Rather, the Yanomama population could be experiencing "a natural deficit of births of female children [which] makes the disproportion between the two sexes more pronounced" (Lizot 1977:504).

Anthropologists' discussions of Yanomama warfare, abuse of women, and female infanticide allow for widely differing opinions and conclusions. In Chagnon's interpretation, Yanomama mothers collude in their own oppression by killing their daughters—an act that unwittingly creates a shortage of women for whom aggressive men must therefore compete and fight. This situation promotes violence, as men argue over women, who are in short supply. Chagnon assumed that Yanomama women accept this male-defined ideology of "worthless" females and "valuable" males. Harris (1974:103) elaborated this theme in his analysis of Yanomama warfare. By contrast, Lizot and Ramos challenged these misogynous views of Yanomama women, including the premise that women are to blame for men's aggressive outrages.[11]

The Shapeless Shrew and Experienced Matron. To conclude our discussion of the anthropological romance of the Wild Woman as primitive, let us consider two descriptions of Yanomama women. After cataloguing numerous incidents of male abuse of women, Chagnon (1977:83) wrote:

> It is not difficult to understand, then, why Yąnomamö women in general have such a vindictive and caustic attitude toward the external world. By the time a woman is thirty years old she has "lost her shape" and has developed a rather unpleasant disposition. Women tend to seek refuge and consolation in each other's company, sharing their misery with their peers.

Lizot (1976a:97), who has worked for many years with the Yanomama, stated that women

> form solidary groups, informally directed by one or more older women who guide them in the search for fruit, the collecting of frogs or insects, crab hunting; these matrons have experience, they are good councilors. The women have their little secrets, their magic, their reserved domains, they provide mutual aid and are irreplaceable in the economic life of the community. [our translation]

Are Yanomama women "unpleasant," shapeless, and oppressed victims? Do they have mutually supportive relationships among themselves? Or do they seek other women's company to commiserate their common denigration?

We neither attempt to reconcile these differing views of Yanomama women nor to declare one "wrong" and the other "right." We are not concerned here with ethnographic "truth." Rather, by tracing recurring images of Yanomama women, we have asked the question: Whose perspective is presented?

Images of the Wild Woman convey sexuality and exploitation in anthropological accounts of gender relations. Constrained by her reproductive functions, the primitive woman unleashes her physical urges and sexual passions. She constitutes actual or potential trouble for men by questioning, disregarding, or subverting male interests in a multitude of ways. Thus, the Wild Woman has latent powers to discomfort or harm men, but, theoretically, she can be harnessed. From a misogynist's perspective, the nature of women is to nurture men and to provoke them. Men, therefore, are expected to respond to women with power and violence. Anthropological literature incorporates the ambivalent forces that the Wild Woman arouses by her body and by her presence in the lives of men. Yet anthropology relegates the Wild Woman to the periphery. Capable of provoking men's lust and prowess, she stands outside the political and ideological boundaries of her own society.

Politics involve women in Nuer, Tiwi, and Yanomama societies. However, political processes are considered men's business. Nuer men are depicted as asserting political and social control over female sexuality and childbearing. Paralleling colonial concerns with relations between rulers and the ruled, Nuer men exercise political and legal rights over women's bodies, labor, and issue in Evans-Pritchard's analysis. Male violence and sexual politics are implicit forces operating in Evans-Pritchard's account of the Nuer, and they are explicit factors in Chagnon's analysis of the Yanomama. Men rape, mutilate, and beat women, according to Chagnon and Harris's interpretations of Chagnon's observations. The savage male unleashes hostility against women, described as bad tempered and shapeless. Nonetheless, Yanomama women are thought to instigate male aggression and warfare by their sexual allure. Similarly, Tiwi women are thought to collude in their own exploitation. It is women who arouse their husbands' anger against other men by acting promiscuously. The reader is led to believe that Yanomama and Tiwi men would live harmoniously if their Wild Women could be controlled. Wild Women, then, are portrayed as deserving the punishments they receive from men.

Selective prisms of sex and gender complicate the social and personal dynamics of anthropological fieldwork. Confronting the Nuer as an outsider and stranger, Evans-Pritchard was the fieldworker—the "marginal man" whom the Nuer treated with suspicion. Evans-Pritchard (1940a:9) claimed he had no regular informants; his understanding of Nuer society, disrupted by colonial pacification and cattle disease, was primarily based on observing men's behavior. Submerged in his observations are images of the Nuer Wild Woman, who surfaces briefly when she is transformed into a man—either as a female husband or as a genealogical link, treated as if she were male. Information on Nuer women must be carefully gleaned and separated from androcentric concern with patrilineal descent, men's legal rights over women and cattle, and the bewildering political processes of "ordered anarchy" involving Nuer men.

Tiwi men in Hart and Pilling's ethnography are financial wizards in the currency of women. As jokester and gamester, the Tiwi male plays his trumps by arranging marriage transactions and by acquiring wives, who may be virgins, widows, or "toothless old hags." Accordingly, Wild Women in Tiwi society are objectified and debased.

Erstwhile primitives in a world of mission stations, trade goods, schools, introduced diseases, mining interests, and even tourists, the Yanomama are interpreted by Chagnon through a Hobbesian vision of brutishness and violence.[12] Such views have led to convictions that indigenous peoples are worthy of extermination (Billington 1981:25–28; Davis 1977:1–18). Woman-hating dominates Yanomama social relations in Chagnon's and Harris's accounts. Using a model of the ignoble savage in the atavistic tropics, men's brutality against women is explained by functionalist interrelations of warfare, sexual competition, and the artificially created scarcity of women. Ultimately, the recalcitrant Wild Woman is to blame for the devastation agents of Western contact visit upon the Yanomama.

4. The Virgin and the Amazon

> *I am a wild woman,*
> *from the deep, deep mora bush,*
> *from the high, high mountain top.*
> *I am going to carry someone away.*
> *I wonder who it will be.*[1]
>
> Carib Indian Song, Guyana

"In the beginning all the world was America," wrote John Locke in 1690.[2] Vast potential was waiting in the new land, according to *The Second Treatise of Civil Government* (Locke 1690), and it would go to waste unless seized and turned into property.[3] By means of their enterprise, civilized men could succeed in the task of transforming America from a state of chaotic nature into an orderly society. With these notions, Locke sketched an attitude that accompanied perceptions of America as unexplored and exploitable. Inhabited by primitive savages—childlike, naive, natural—the New World awaited penetration by civilized men who would reveal its secrets which lay ripe for discovery.

In European eyes America was simultaneously known and unknown. America offered youthful renewal, and it also represented the past. Clothed in exotic flora and fauna, inhabited by primitives, the New World provided scope for utopian visions and fantasies of regaining paradise lost. The New World proffered an agenda of desiderata. In the projective imagination of the Old World, America was antediluvian but pristine, virginal but erotic, wild but tameable.

Moreover, America was female. America in the sixteenth century was depicted as a dusky, supine figure accompanied by tropical fauna and cornucopias of abundance. Cannibalism and gold-seeking were recurrent themes portrayed about her. The exotic and savage became one in these allegorical illustrations of America as woman, while erotica and cupidity for gold were linked in the metaphor of America as a state of archaic female nature:

> Personified as an Indian woman, usually scantily clad in feathers, surrounded by heaps of gold coins and pearls and exotic wildlife like parrots, armadillos and alligators, the allegorical America was a dazzling, ripe image of the wealth Europe dreamed of possessing, as indeed it did as the colonial rulers of most of the New World. (Trachtenberg 1976:28)

Fabulous wealth for the taking was portrayed by the tropical Indian maiden. Vulnerable, childlike, nude, mute, presocial, timeless, and sexually promising, the New World as virgin symbolized personal fantasy. Through her, men hoped to recreate an infantile past and fulfill egoistic demands. The symmetry among the conquest, rape, and plunder of the New World was inescapable.[4]

The identity of America as native female waiting to be ravaged is a persistent theme in the writings of early explorers. These projected images of exotica and erotica surrounding the New World comprise an intellectual legacy that counterposes the masculine, civilized self with the feminine, savage other. In this chapter we examine the Romance of the New World as Wild Woman portrayed in historical, literary, and anthropological sources.

AMERICA AS WOMAN

The notion of the earth or land as female has a long tradition in the Western world. It derives from an understanding of nature as a female organism in contrast to human society as a male domain. With the economic transformation of Europe during the sixteenth and seventeenth centuries, the theme of dominating mother earth emerged as an enabling premise for economic enterprise. The image of man mastering earth as a female body acquired special meanings as it was projected onto the New World.

In the fantasies of the unknown New World, the sexuality of the female earth is chaotic and destructive. Rather than being a nurturing, maternal figure, she is sexually provocative. America, incarnate as the aboriginal female, is the lure—ever out of reach and begging exploration. The image of the Wild Woman as America promising erotic delights is a prologue to conquest in which European men invited themselves through sexual metaphors of lust and mastery.

The Torrid Zone

For Europeans, the discovery of unknown regions stimulated ideas about the earth as female. During his third voyage, Christopher Columbus ([1493–1506] 1961:130) wrote:

> I have come to another conclusion respecting the earth, namely, that it is not round as they describe, but of the form of a pear, which is very round except where the stalk grows, at which part it is most prominent; or like a round ball, upon one part of which is a prominence like a woman's nipple, this protrusion being the highest and nearest the sky, situated under the equinoctial line, and at the eastern extremity of this sea. . . .

If the earth was like a woman's body, then the regions yet to be discovered were her sexual parts.

Columbus further exaggerated the sexuality of the New World by its proximity to the sun. The tropics were viewed with expectations of fantastic excitement during Columbus's day, since the heat of the sun was thought to be like the heat of sexual passion. Columbus's perception also drew from a medieval idea that the Garden of Eden, where Adam and Eve needed no clothes, was located on the highest point of the earth untouched by Noah's flood (McCann 1951:22).

Thus, innocent sexuality, an earthly paradise in the tropics, and gold to be found in America as woman were woven together.

In the beginning, of course, Europeans had no name for America. The voyages of Christopher Columbus, Pedro Alvares Cabral, and others brought reports of land masses across the sea, and many believed that the distant shore of Asia had been reached. Assuming he had found a sea route to India, Columbus wrote about "Indians" encountered in the new land. Similarly, Cabral sought access to trade in spices from India. However, in time it became apparent that, in addition to Europe, Africa, and Asia, a fourth part of the world existed.

Voyages continued and information accumulated. In the town of Saint-Die in Lorraine, mapmakers in the early years of the sixteenth century prepared a new edition of Ptolemy's *Geography*. Among them, geographer Martin Waldseemüller in 1507 produced a map in which "America" was affixed to the newly discovered world (Honour 1975:12–13). Its namesake, Amerigo Vespucci, a Florentine adventurer, was one among many who made the trip to the new land. It is usually assumed that only by an accident of history did his feminized name come to be attached to the New World.

Vespucci sailed during 1501 and 1502 to the coast of South America. He later wrote about this voyage to his patron, Lorenzo Pietro di Medici. This letter, along with others, was published in Latin, Italian, German, and Dutch and gained wide circulation. One aspect of the Vespucci correspondence stands out—attention to the sexuality of women in the new continent:

> The women as I have said go about naked and are very libidinous; yet they have bodies which are tolerably beautiful and cleanly. Nor are they so unsightly as one perchance might imagine; for, inasmuch as they are plump, their ugliness is the less apparent, which indeed is for the most part concealed by the excellence of their bodily structure. It was to us a matter of astonishment that none was to be seen among them who had a flabby breast, and those who had borne children were not to be distinguished from virgins by the shape and

shrinking of the womb; and in the other parts of the body similar things were seen of which in the interest of modesty I make no mention. When they had the opportunity of copulating with Christians, urged by excessive lust, they defiled and prostituted themselves. They live one hundred and fifty years, and rarely fall ill, and if they do fall victims to any disease, they cure themselves with certain roots and herbs. These are the most noteworthy things I know about them. (Vespucci [1503] 1916a:7)

Thus, from among many possible candidates, the New World was named for Amerigo Vespucci, who drew from the projective imagination of Europe a sensational portrayal of erotic women inhabiting the newly discovered tropics.

Vespucci's interest in the sexuality of New World women underscored a prurient inversion of the European social order. In addition to enjoying sex without shame, Vespucci's letters continued, New World women are fertile, their pregnancies are easy, and parturition causes no inconvenience. Moreover, American Indian women are sadistic and immoral; they know how to enlarge their lovers' penises by applying venomous insects, which can be lethal, and they also understand the secrets of inducing miscarriage and controlling their fertility despite their husbands' wishes. These women are capable warriors and cannibals, yet they remain simple children of nature. In a letter to Piero Soderini, Vespucci ([1504] 1916b:9) wrote:

> Their wealth consists of feathers of many-hued birds, or of little rosaries which they make out of fish bones, or of white or green stones which they stick through cheeks, lips, and ears, and of many other things to which we attach no value. They engage in no barter (whatsoever); they neither buy nor sell. In short, they live and are contented with what nature gives them. The wealth which we affect in this our Europe and elsewhere, such as gold, jewels, pearls, and other riches, they hold of no value at all; and although they have them in their lands they do not work to get them, nor do they care for them.

These mythologized descriptions of the New World reveal a great deal about early sixteenth-century Europe. Desiring profit and preoccupied with Old World social restrictions, Europeans projected the inversion of their own world onto an unknown land and the people within it. In particular, the women of that remote land came to symbolize all that the New World promised.

The New World presented an extreme contrast to orderly existence in Europe. Michael de Montaigne's ([1580] 1935:170) autobiography described the New World as a state of negation:

> It is a nation with no kind of commerce; no knowledge of letters or numbers; no name of magistrate or political superiority; no wealth, poverty, or need of servants; no contracts, inheritance, or division of property. . . .

Contrary to temperate Europe, America was the southern continent, the "Torrid Zone" about which Vespucci had written. Moreover, the indigenes and especially the women found in this lush, primeval setting were a part of nature conceived as atavistic and unruled. The most anticipated characteristic of these newly found natural women was their overt sexuality. Erotica, chaos, and gold of the tropics were fused into a powerful metaphor—the New World as woman, unexplored and vulnerable. She was a void; she was what man was not. Everything that existed in the known world was null in her, and yet she was desired for the sumptuous delights and bountiful treasures that civilized men assumed she promised.

Mining for Gold: The Earth as Woman's Body. The widely held notion during the Middle Ages that the sun's rays could engender gold in the earth encouraged alchemists to attempt to replicate the process and forge gold out of base metals. The force of the sun's rays was thought to bring about gold "veins" in the earth analogous to those of the female body, while the motherload of gold was to be found in the earth's womb. Mining was thought to be a violation of mother earth; men would dig in her secret places where precious substances were hidden (Merchant 1980:1–41).

The logic connecting heat, gold, and mother earth also pointed to the tropics as the place to find the precious metal—hence the sixteenth-century belief that the region between the Tropic of Cancer and the Tropic of Capricorn held vast quantities of gold (McCann 1951:3–14).

The idea of mother earth became virgin earth in the search for gold in the New World. Gold mining was to the earth as rape was to the woman. Gold evoked avarice, which was compared to lust. This analogy mystified and excited both desires. Identity and survival were at stake in the "gold fever" accompanying the search for the precious metal, understood as sexual penetration of virgin soil.

During their search for gold, men returned to the creation of the earth as the first, or Golden Age. Later periods were separated from this primordial bliss, with a Silver Age succeeded by the Bronze and Tin Ages. Hence the quest for gold was also a dangerous return to the beginning and the primitive simplicity of a Golden Age, which America represented (Levin 1969). This Golden Age of innocent origins was sought through the sexual conquest of virgin earth.

Sexual License and Utopia in the New World

Like the earth's erotic zones, the tropical New World promoted the linkage of sexuality with a conscious return to the Golden Age. The New World was free for the taking; eros was unshackled from the restraints and responsibilities of civilized existence in the Old World. The stage was therefore set for utopian dreams.

One of the earliest quests for New World romance was described by Sir Thomas More, who located his paradise on an island off the coast of tropical South America. Hytholday, a Portuguese sailor who supposedly left Vespucci's expedition to venture further into the New World, is the narrator of More's *Utopia*, published in 1516. Told in Peter Giles's garden in Antwerp, the story relates the marvels of this imagined place where the lust for possessions, the root of evil in existing societies, is overcome. Property is abolished and social equality is established in More's perfect world. In a reference to the disgust for wealth Vespucci found among New World inhabitants, the chamber pots in *Utopia* are made of gold. Concupiscence and desire for earthly pleasures are dismissed as unworthy. Thus, the pleasures of the mind, holding the greatest promise for contentment, rank above those of the body, while intellectual pursuits are guided by attaining the greatest delights without bringing pain or harm to others.

More's utopian vision reveals the emerging social charter of sixteenth- and seventeenth-century Europe by projecting its reverse onto a hypothetical society of the New World. Critical to both worlds are pleasure and treasure and the means to attain them. Wealth understood as the greatest felicity and mental contentment is the inversion of wealth as monetary gain and capital accumulation. Money versus happiness is the primary dualism, as men measure themselves in reference to each other.

More ([1516] 1904:70) paid little attention to gender relations in *Utopia*, although a great deal is revealed about women's assigned place:

> The men sit upon the bench next the wall, and the women against them on the other side of the table, that, if any sudden evil should chance to them, as many times happens to women with child, they may rise without trouble or disturbance of anybody, and go thence into the nurcery.

Presumably women perform their domestic duties, absorb social tensions, and quietly bear and rear children so that men are free to engage in utopian endeavors.

As America was explored, other writers focused on Guyana as an inversion of the known.[5] The English bishop, Joseph Hall, in *Satire III* ([1597] 1824:91), commented: "Venturous Fortunio his farm has sold, and gads to Guiane land to fish for gold." In Hall's version, the adventurer is contrasted with another who stays at home and explores alchemy to obtain vast treasure. John Donne, the English preacher and poet, included "Guianaes rarities" in a list of the bizarre, along with African monsters, life engendered in Nilotic slime, and antiquarian studies in *Satyre IV* ([1633] 1929:131). The seventeenth-century English poet, Michael Drayton, celebrated in *Poly-Olbion* ([1612–22] 133:406) the English countryside with the contrasting image of Guyana as "the land (by nature's power) with wonders most repleat." In *Paradise Lost,* John Milton ([1667] 1840:284) described Guyana as "yet unspoiled" but awaiting imminent corruption. Guyana, then, existed in the literary imagination as an earthly, vulnerable paradise with the potential for generating amazing creatures and yielding precious treasures.

GUYANA AS UNEXPLORED VIRGIN

Examined in the sequence of contact, the feminine labeling of the New World reveals a pattern. At first the entire tropical New World is thought of as a virgin, but, after subsequent exploration, only unknown regions within it are perceived in this way. Untold treasure and pleasure are kept in an ideological reserve for the adventures of men. The interior rain forest of Guyana, one of its least-known regions, endures the image of a waiting maiden.

Walter Raleigh's Maid

After the failure of Virginia, the American colony named for his virgin queen, Walter Raleigh turned his efforts to the little-known region of South America. Able to read Spanish travel reports and maps, Raleigh was well acquainted with the European quest for El Dorado, an earthly paradise (Bauden [1965] 1976:33). Raleigh embraced the myth of colossal, undiscovered wealth in the New World and pursued rumors of a New Dorado on the eastern coast of South America in territory unsecured by the Spanish (Payne 1900:xxiv-xxv).

After reconnoitering in Guyana, Raleigh subsequently wrote *The Discovery of the Large, Rich, and Beautiful Empire of Guiana* (1596), designed to promote royal support for his expeditions. Filled with phantasmagoria, Raleigh's ([1596]

1848:82) account crystallized the vision of Guyana in the English mind:

> I never saw a more beautiful country, nor more likely prospects, hills so raised here and there over the valleys, the river winding into divers branches, the plains adjoining without bush or stubble, all fair green grass, the ground of hard sand easy to march on, either for horse or foot, the deer crossing in every path, the birds towards the evening singing on every tree with a thousand several tunes, cranes and herons of white, crimson, and carnation perching on the riverside, the air fresh with a gently easterly wind, and every stone that we stopped to take up, promised either gold or silver by its complexion.

The idyllic paradise of unknown Guyana was conveyed in extravagant images and expectations. Beautiful nature is linked with gold and silver for the taking. In a biography of Sir Walter Raleigh, Henry David Thoreau (1905:36), himself a nineteenth-century prophet of utopian ventures, commented on the image of the New World: "Its mineral wealth was reported to be as inexhaustable as the cupidity of its discoverers was unbounded."

Raleigh ([1596] 1848:82) personified the New World as a virgin promising treasure and pleasure:

> To conclude, *Guiana* is a country that has yet her maidenhead never sacked, turned, nor wrought, the face of the earth has not been torn, nor the virtue and salt of the soil spent by manurance [cultivation], the graves have not been opened for gold, the mines not broken with sledges, nor their images pulled down out of their temples. It has never been entered by any army of strength, and never conquered or possessed by any Christian prince. (emphasis in original)

Lawrence Kemys, a member of Raleigh's first expedition, led a second one sponsored by Raleigh. In the preface to Kemys's book, *A Relation of the Second Voyage to Guiana* (1596), another use of the image of Guyana as woman occurs in a poem, "De Guiana, Carmen Epicum," attributed to George Chapman:

> Guiana, whose rich feet are mines of gold,
> Whose forehead knocks against the roof of stars,
> Stands on her tip-toes at fair England looking
> Kissing her hand, bowing her mighty breast,
> And every figure of all submission making,
> To be her sister, and the daughter both
> Of our most sacred maid; whose barrenness
> Is the true fruit of virtue, that may get,
> Bear and bring forth anew in all perfection,
> What heretofore savage corruption held
> In barbarous chaos; and in this affair
> Become her father, mother, and her heir.
> ([Chapman] 1596:[i])

Guyana, the submissive and bountiful woman, becomes sister and daughter to England. But of the two virgins, one civilized and the other wild, Guyana will be conquered and exploited to benefit England.

The Hidden Amazon

The depiction of Guyana as woman ready to be ravaged was not without ambivalence and foreboding. The helpless, nubile maiden also provoked the counterimage of the warlike, fearless Amazon. While the virgin is naive and willing to please, the Amazon is experienced and dangerous. Their origins lost in the recesses of classical antiquity, Amazons were thought to be as capricious as the fates in store for the hapless men who encountered them (see Kleinbaum 1983). Central to the Amazon myth is the notion of women who lure and then kill their male sex partners.

On his first voyage, Columbus ([1493–1506] 1961:15) was told that a remote island in the Caribbean was inhabited by warlike women. In his exploration during 1541 and 1542 of the Amazon River, which he named, Francisco de Orellana reported indigenous warriors who included women in the front lines. Many other reports of Amazons occur in the early chronicles of tropical America, and recurrently their abode was thought to be in an ever more remote and unreachable region—the interior of Guyana.

Referring to the Amazons of antiquity, Raleigh ([1596] 1848:28) reported:

> But they which are not far from *Guiana* do accompany with men but once in a year, and for the time of one month, which I gather by their relation to be in April. At that time all the kings of the borders assemble, and the queens of the *Amazons* and after the queens have chosen, the rest cast lots for their *valentines*. This one month, they feast, dance, and drink of their wines in abundance, and the moon being done, they all depart to their own provinces. If they conceive, and be delivered of a son, they return him to the father, if of a daughter they nourish it, and retain it, and as many as have daughters send unto the begetters a present, all being desirous to increase their own sex and kind, but that the cut of the right dug of the breast I do not find to be true. It was further told me, that if in the wars they took any prisoners that they used to accompany with those also at what time soever, but in the end for certain they put them to death: for they are said to be very cruel and bloodthirsty, especially to such as offer to invade their territories. (emphasis in original)

The Prussian explorer-scholar Robert H. Schomburgk (1848:lvi–lxi) recorded reputed Amazons in the sixteenth-century New World. Finding the notion of Amazons in the tropical New World to be pervasive, Schomburgk (1848:lvi) wrote that "The account of a tribe of Amazons is almost coeval with the discovery of America."

Schomburgk's brother, Richard, during his travels to survey the boundary of Guyana between 1840 and 1844, also noted the widespread legend of fabled Amazons among Indian groups (Schomburgk [1847–48] 1922–23, 2:261–262). In this version of Amazon legends, warlike women work their fields, hunt alone, and invite men to visit them once a year. The sons resulting from these unions are destroyed while the daughters are saved. The ominous Amazon, who takes a homicidal view of her lover, now kills sons instead of returning them to the father. Stationed in Guyana, Reverend Everard Im Thurn (1883:385) explained that the Indians took up from Europeans the idea of the murderous Amazon—an idea that coincided with increasing Western penetration of Guyana's interior during the late nineteenth century.

The vision of the New World virgin was eclipsed from time to time by that of the Amazon. As European exploration and exploitation accelerated, America the Amazon was thought to deserve the fate intended for the New World as woman—rape and conquest. The violence brought to subdue her was justified by her independence and indifference, feminine ploys to attract and lure the unwary male beguiled by dreams of a perfect world.

An Imperfect World. François Marie Arouet de Voltaire parodied European conquests in *Candide, or Optimism* (1759) in which the devastation intended for unknown lands is visited instead upon the traveler-explorers. The young Frenchman Candide and his valet flee the governor of Buenos Aires who detains Mademoiselle Cunégonde, the relative whom Candide desires to marry. As the sun sets in a strange land, Candide and his valet hear women's "cries of pain or of joy": "These sounds came from two girls, stark naked, who were running lightly along the edge of the meadow, while two monkeys followed them and bit their buttocks" (Voltaire [1759] 1961:49). Candide shoots the monkeys, only to learn that they were "the two lovers of these young ladies" as happens among those "who have not received a certain education" (Voltaire [1759] 1961:49–50). Later, the travelers escape being boiled and eaten by the undernourished and undersexed inhabitants, who are outnumbered by the monkeys in this New World turned upside down (see Gerbi 1973:42–45).

Candide and his valet flee again in the direction of Cayenne, or El Dorado. After many travails, the men find a land in which mud and pebbles are golden, and diamonds and rubies are everywhere. They learn that in this lost world people live to more than one hundred and seventy years of age, that all men are priests, that crime is absent, and that all are of one opinion concerning religion. The travelers are eventually sent to see the king of this utopia. Voltaire, who turned his wit to the defense of victims of political inequality, repeated the image of New World women who lure men to avarice, disappointment, and doom. Twenty beautiful women dress the two unsatisfied adventurers in "robes woven from hummingbird down" (Voltaire [1759] 1961:57). Wishing to leave this utopian world where wealth does not distinguish people, Candide and his faithful valet are given more gold and jewels. Carried by sheep, the two men and their loot are hoisted out of the mountain refuge by a contraption invented for the purpose. Candide and his companion, who repair to Buenos Aires to rescue the captive Mademoiselle Cunégonde, meet more adventure and lose their treasure in the less than perfect New World.

Returning to the Old World, the men eventually locate Cunégonde in Transylvania and ransom her:

> The tender lover Candide, on seeing his fair Cunégonde darkskinned, eyes bloodshot, flat-bosomed, cheeks wrinkled, arms red and rough, recoiled three steps in horror, and then advanced out of good manners. (Voltaire [1759] 1961:96–97)

It is discovered that, "at the bottom of his heart, Candide had no desire to marry Cunégonde" (Voltaire [1759] 1961:97). Like all New World women, Cunégonde had quickly aged after her brief flower of youth. She is now very ugly; nevertheless, Candide cannot retreat. They marry and revert to a childlike existence in a Garden of Eden at home where the women are assigned the washing, sewing, and cooking.

The Garden of Wild Women. Civilized men cannot sustain themselves in the feminized tropics of the New World, where disorder and terror prevail. Sir Thomas More ([1516] 1904:5) described the horrors of such places:

> All things be hideous, terrible, loathsome, and unpleasant to behold; all things out of fashion and comeliness; inhabited with wild beasts and serpents, or at the last wise with people that be no less savage, wild, and noisome than the very beasts themselves be.

The tropical New World is unwholesome and hostile, and its inhabitants noxious and sinister.

In a unique utopian vision, Margaret Cavendish, Duchess of Newcastle, wrote *The Description of a New World, Called the Blazing World* (1666). Matter, spirit, reason, and empathy combine in a beneficent realm in which women thoughtfully speak with fish-men and worm-men, among other bizarre entities. Rather than conquer worlds, women create them—worlds "so curious and full of variety, so well ordered and wisely governed, that it cannot possibly be expressed by words" (Cavendish 1666:101). Cavendish's ideas, however, were forgotten (Paloma 1980). Her version of a rational and tranquil New World was obscured by the fearsome views of impending chaos expressed by her male contemporaries.

Other interpretations of a more virtuous New World also lacked authenticity. In her novel *Oroonoko; or, the History of the Royal Slave,* Aphra Behn (1688), the first woman to claim an identity as a writer, portrayed the savage as a noble hero in her account of the ills of slavery along South America's Wild Coast, as Surinam was then called. Behn's contemporaries and subsequent scholars discredited her—as well as her vision of the New World—for more than two centuries, claiming that her book was completely fiction, that she had not written her own work, or that she never existed (Gardiner 1980, Goreau 1980).

By the eighteenth century, European observers regarded the New World as a disappointing failure of utopian fantasies. America was imperfect. Indeed, it was a biological, moral, and social disaster:

> Before the American Revolution a school of distinguished Enlightenment philosophers at odds with Rousseau developed the thesis that America was a "mistake," its discovery a disaster, its influence a curse to mankind. In its abysmal climate and miasmic atmosphere plants, animals, human beings, and society degenerated catastrophically, and in Europe it spread disease, inflation, national rivalries, wars and misery. (Woodward 1981:33)

America was to blame for the ills that accompanied the mercantile transformation of Europe, just as women were and are to blame for the consequences of men's sexual aggression. America could come to no good; likewise, women.

Coincidental with the American and French revolutions, a new view was taken of America. The eighteenth-century romance with the primitive transformed the wild man from a debased menace into the noble savage of the New World (H. White 1972). However, by the nineteenth century the noble savage was rendered inferior by the attribution of feminine qualities. According to this romantic revision of nature, nobility belonged to the adventurer who conquered other worlds, rather than to their aboriginal inhabitants. The explorer calmed the fear of being surpassed by those of worthy character by making the primitive a woman. She was rude and sensual. Thus, it was possible, indeed, it was comfortable for Europeans to view the vast potential of the New World and to insist on its fundamental impotence. Accordingly, the philosopher Georg Friedrich Hegel ([1837] 1975:164) described the peoples of South America as lacking vigor: "One must read the accounts of travellers to appreciate their mildness and passivity, their humility and obsequious submissiveness towards a Creole [person of mixed aboriginal and Old World backgrounds], and even more towards a European." Even the animals inhabiting the New World are diminished. Lions, tigers, and crocodiles are feeble runts in this realm of "unenlightened children, living from one day to the next, and untouched by higher thoughts or aspirations" (Hegel [1837] 1975:165). According to this view, America had stagnated at some earlier stage. It was an antediluvian world in suspension. Meanwhile, Europeans were busy accomplishing their goals, which included conquering the New World and upholding their roles in history.

THE RAIN FOREST AND THE FECUND MOTHER

By mid-nineteenth century, the feminine chaos of nature could no longer be kept at a distance from civilized society. Charles Darwin's theory of natural selection, which explained the creation of new species in a vocabulary of struggle and conquest, disturbed notions of man's relation to nature. Only the fittest survive to reproduce in "the great battle for life" (Darwin ([1859] 1866:156). For both Darwin and Alfred Wallace, who independently formulated the theory of natural selection, travel to the American tropics as naturalists was critical in developing their views about the variability of life forms and their struggle for survival. The legacy of the American tropics as female, with untold generative potential to produce amazing progeny, profoundly influenced Darwin and Wallace, who perceived that all the world, like America, was in a state of nature.

Zoological Exotica

In contrast to the zoological tidiness of Europe, animal life in the New World, particularly Guyana, was thought to be rampant and to take forms beyond imagination. England acquired Guyana in 1814. Eleven years later naturalist Charles Waterton explored this territory and introduced it to English readers in his book, *Wanderings in South America* (1825). Waterton described the natural marvels of the jungle: jaguars, gigantic alligators, voracious vampire bats, immense snakes, electric eels, piranhas, and unidentified flora and fauna.

> The wild beasts, snakes, the swamps, the trees, the uncurbed luxuriance of everything around you, conspire to inform you that man has no habitation here—man has seldom passed this way. (Waterton [1825] 1909:213)

Guyana was pristine; it was a woman, or a no-man's-land. Like a woman, Guyana is seductive. At the outset of his third journey, Waterton ([1825] 1909:168) mused: "Guiana still whispered in my ear, and seemed to invite me once more to wander through her distant forests."

Waterton's natural history repeated the theme expressed in sixteenth-century England: Guyana was a wellspring of nature's chaotic marvels, as opposed to the orderly, hierarchic society of men. Guyanese novelist Jan Carew (1958:112) echoed this idea by describing the rain forest as "a womb in which life is lived in an eternal, dark gestation, only the undulating belly of treetops is exposed."

Biologist Charles Beebe, in *Jungle Peace* (1919), portrayed the forest of Guyana as a natural world in delicate balance. Fifty years later anthropologist Betty J. Meggers, in *Amazonia: Man and Culture in a Counterfeit Paradise* (1971), called attention to the intricate ecology of the South American rain forest and its vulnerability to Western technologies. The forest and its natural phenomena are considered female; nature is either a fecund mother or a sleeping, fragile maiden who proves less innocent than originally conceived.

Loathsome and Barbarous Women. Naturalists also studied the people of Guyana's interior landscape while recording nature's mysteries. Richard Schomburgk ([1847–48] 1922–23, 1:94) surveyed the interior boundaries of Guyana between 1840 and 1844 and described the Warrau Indian women he found there:

> When the female reaches her twentieth year, the bloom of her life is spent: the former symmetry of her individual limbs and figure has disappeared, the elasticity of all her movements has given way to a certain indolence, and in place of a vitally fresh and robust fulness there appears on particular parts of the body an accumulation of fat which makes her really loathsome, because no clothing hides the misshapen masses from view.

Sexually active at an early age, these "indolent" women rapidly decline into repulsiveness. Existing in a state of nature, they make obvious the inevitable decrepitude of all women.

Similarly, Reverend William H. Brett (1868:121), missionary to Guyana in the mid-1800s, described Carib Indian women:

> The appearance of those women was very barbarous, as is indeed the case with most of the Caribi females. Their dress was merely a narrow strip of blue cloth, and their naked bodies were smeared

with the red arnotto [a plant-derived pigment], which gave them the appearance of bleeding from every pore. As if this were not sufficiently ornamental, some of them had endeavoured to improve its appearance by blue spots upon their bodies and limbs.

Brett (1868:122) viewed ankle and knee bands as distorting these women's calves from youth, while sewing pins carried in perforations of the lower lip were described as "the most singular part of their appearance."

Carib women also attracted the attention of Lieutenant Colonel George Daniel Webber and his party, traveling along the Essequibo River en route to the newly-discovered Kaieteur Falls:

> Young and old they all wore tight leathern straps, coloured red with arnatto, about four inches wide, below the knee and above the ankle. These were their only clothes, if we except a string round the waist with a pendant apron of beads six inches square in front. (Webber 1873:10)

Webber (1873:9–11) found these "ill-favoured squaws," as he called them, to be "ugly as Satan":

> These women had pins stuck into their lips and nostrils—perhaps to prevent liberties! but the cocoanut and crab oil with which they besmeared was a "military obstacle" at once. Hannibal and his elephants were a joke to it! (Webber 1873:10)

Naked and repulsive, Carib women suffer in these descriptions as "squaws" unworthy of civilized men's approval.

A dialectic of desire and denigration emerged with regard to the indigenous women of Guyana. Imagined as alluring and magical, they are alternately virgins or Amazons. However, these early observers' search for the reality of their projections inevitably resulted in disappointment. American Indian women, "loathsome" and "barbarous," are denigrated when civilized men discover neither perfect maidens nor demonic Amazons.

Reverend Brett also collected Indian tales and presented them in rhymed verse in *Legends and Myths of the Aboriginal*

Indians of British Guiana (1880). In one myth, Korobana, a young woman, is held captive by a spirit whose sexual desire she awakens. Korobana subsequently gives birth to a child whom she tries to protect from her brothers:

> "Kill not my baby girl," she cries;
> "Slay *me*—the mad and wild!
> But she a gentle maid will be,
> And serve you all most lovingly.
> O spare the helpless child!"
> (Brett 1880:66, emphasis in original)

Korobana, the "mad and wild," is transformed by her ripe sexuality into a wanton female like those thought to inhabit the forests and waters of the interior in other mythological tales (Brett 1868:367-379). Korobana is replaced by her virgin daughter, ready to repeat the process.

This virgin/Amazon continuum is an ideological ambush for the real woman. Neither a promising virgin nor a mythical Amazon, she is mundane, vulgar, and lacks magical powers to excite the male who encounters her. Failing to be a martyr, the real woman is unremarkable to men, especially when she is encountered in the tropical forests of Guyana, the expected abode of virgins and Amazons.

Her best remaining role is that of nurse, when needed. "Old Jeannette," for example (Brett 1881:6–20), was a house slave on a plantation in Guyana. After emancipation, Jeannette moved to a missionary station in the forest, where Indian parents occasionally left schoolchildren in her care. She tenderly nursed the young missionary Brett, like one of her charges, when he fell ill with a tropical fever. Jeannette eventually met death in an unfortunate marriage to an abusive black man greedy for her few possessions.

Women as Flora and Fauna

James Rodway's book, *In the Guiana Forest: Studies of Nature in Relation to the Struggle for Life* (1894), continued to catalogue the natural history of Guyana. Convinced of Darwinian processes of struggle and sexual fitness, he wrote: "nowhere can we study man as an animal so well as in the Guiana forest" (Rodway 1894:19). Rodway, in the novel *In Guiana Wilds: A Study of Two Women* (1899), extended his naturalist's views to the examination of women living in the forest. Allen, a young Scot employed as a clerk in Georgetown, the colonial capital, vacations in the interior, where he is saved from drowning by the native Miss Chloe. He sees her as an angel, and after a night together in the bush, he saves her by marriage. Back in Georgetown, Allen feels compromised by Chloe's mixed black and Indian heritage. Moreover, Chloe demands a style of life beyond a clerk's means. Pressed by creditors, the young husband dreams he is immobilized as a snake coils around his leg, glares into his eyes, and bites his cheek.

After Chloe gives birth to a daughter and the bailiffs carry off their furniture, Allen flees to the interior. There he joins a group of Indians returning to the deep bush, where his dreams about a vengeful mother-monster continue to unsettle him:

> If he dozed for a few minutes, it was to dream of his wife. At one time she was following him with an Indian club; she had stripped herself, and had become the dreaded Kenaima, the avenger of blood. Her lovely body was painted with spots like those of the jaguar, and her eyes were balls of fire. He ran from her into the forests, but she followed him everywhere. (Rodway 1899:110–111)

Allen lives with the Indians and acquires another wife, a submissive "flower" who "bore caresses but never gave them in return" (Rodway 1899:143). While Allen's first wife changes into a menacing animal that pursues him, his second wife tries to "keep beyond his reach" (Rodway 1899:143). In the course of events, Allen and his wife of the forest become refugees in the bush. They flee from a serpent-like avenger of the Indian people, the repulsive, sexually consuming Kanaima who attacks the lone male. In this case, Kanaima is also the personification of Allen's first wife, Chloe, the virgin transformed into the monstrous Amazon.

The Virgin as Vermin. Naturalist William Henry Hudson also tried his hand at writing novels about the tropics and its Wild Women. *Green Mansions: A Romance of the Tropical Forest* was first published in England in 1904. The novel details Mr. Abel's fantastic story of Rima, "a wild, solitary girl of the woods" who is a "tantalizing, elusive, mysterious creature" (Hudson [1904] 1944:69, 88). Hudson described Rima in much the same manner as he described the wildlife in his natural history books of South America. Like an exotic bird, Rima's skin and hair are of luminous, changing hues. She is graced with a melodious voice and a "birdlike wildness" (Hudson [1904] 1944:88). Alternately, Rima seems to be an insect. In her irridescent garment spun by spiders, she is "free as the butterfly" (Hudson [1904] 1944:88). When the Indians set fire to the tree in which she hides, Rima is likened to "a great white bird killed with an arrow." As she falls to the ground, she is "burnt to ashes like a moth in the flames of a fire" (Hudson [1904] 1944:218).

> The Indians regarded Rima with fear and hatred: She was constantly in the woods frustrating them; and the animals, in league with her, seemed to understand her note of warning and hid themselves or took to flight at the appearance of danger. (Hudson [1904] 1944:177)

Moreover, it was rumored that Rima, not unlike the mythic Amazon, caught arrows with her hands and hurled them back with deadly aim at the marksman. The Indians believed that

> the mysterious girl who could not be shot was the offspring of an old man and a Didi who had become enamoured of him; that, growing tired of her consort, the Didi had returned to her river, leaving her half-human child to play her malicious pranks in the wood. (Hudson [1904] 1944:177)

In the folklore of Guyanese Indians, a *di-di* is an evil being—part monkey and part woman—who lives in the deep forest near the river bank (Im Thurn 1883:385). A *di-di* intercepts lone men by appearing in tantalizing forms and leads them to their deaths.

Rima, the child of a human-*di-di* union, is burned, since "there is no way to kill her except by fire" (Hudson [1904] 1944:217). Rima's fate contrasts with that of the English woman Abel has left behind:

> A daughter of civilisation and of that artificial life, she could never experience such feelings as these and return to nature as I was doing. For women, though within narrow limits more plastic than men, are yet without that larger adaptiveness which can take us back to the sources of life, which they have left externally behind. Better, far better for both of us that she should wait through the long, slow months, growing sick at heart with hope deferred; that, seeing me no more, she should weep my loss, and be healed at last by time, and find love and happiness again in the old way, in the old place. (Hudson [1904] 1944:111–112)

Between the tameable virgin and the untractable Amazon emerges the English woman—domestic and uninspiring. Both the dull English woman and the fantastic Indian woman suffer denigration when men discover them to be other than envisioned.

The extension of animal names to women reveals an important dynamic of their social ostracism. The female called by a "pet" name is malleable, a private playmate. She may be an adorable kitten or bunny, someone who absorbs the personal attentions of her master. A woman called by the name of an exotic wild animal is thought to be beyond human control; she is a tigress or a bitch, independent and unresponsive. Between these two distinctions lies a zone of vulgarity: to call a woman a "cow" or "pig" indicts her for being domestic and tame. In this ideological system, women are denigrated as virgins to be possessed, Amazons worthy of conquest, or neither of these. The character of Rima in *Green Mansions* is the Wild Woman who is made one man's pet. The Indians, however, interpret her as a pest, a predatory bird. The virgin becomes vermin, a noxious insect. Exciting pleasure as a virgin, Rima subsequently provokes danger and excitement as a pest. She is exterminated.[6]

THE PRIMEVAL WOMAN WITHIN

Twentieth-century literature explores themes of psychological interiors through personal quests into the Guyanese rain forest. Novelists draw on the powerful metaphors of Guyana as woman who offers treasure/pleasure, while the tropics as virgin reappear as the Amazon.

The Hidden World of Wild Women

Among Guyanese Indians, any inaccessible rock is thought to be inhabited by monstrous animals (Im Thurn 1883:385). Sir Arthur Conan Doyle's novel, *The Lost World* (1912), combined this idea with the theme that danger lurks in the silent luxuriance of the tropics. Ape-men, primitives, and superhumans interact in the presence of pterodactyls and dinosaurs on a plateau in the Guyanese frontier.

In order to prove himself a man of action and experience, newspaper reporter Malone joins an expedition led by Professor Challenger. Hoping to impress Gladys, a young Englishwoman who has so far remained aloof, Malone laments:

> That delicately bronzed skin, almost Oriental in its colouring, that raven hair, the large liquid eyes, the full but exquisite lips—all the stigmata of passion were there. But I was sadly conscious that up to now I have never found the secret of drawing it forth. (Doyle 1912:4–5)

Gladys is self-sufficient, "chirpy," and "emancipated" (Pearsall 1977:130). By conquering the primeval world, Malone believes he will also conquer Gladys, who has stayed behind in England. After circling the plateau for six days, the expedition scales an adjacent precipice and crosses over felled trees to encounter the ape-men.

In 1912, the same year that *The Lost World* was published, the discovery of *Eoanthropus dawsoni* was announced to the Geological Society of London. Doyle lived eight miles from the village of Piltdown and the nearby gravel quarry in Sussex County where Piltdown Man, as it became known, was found. Doyle visited the excavation site and expressed interest in what was considered to be the earliest known human fossil. Subsequently, scientists revealed Piltdown Man, comprised of a human skull with an orangutan mandible, to be an elaborate fake. Many years earlier, English naturalist Charles Waterton ([1825] 1909:302–304) brought back from Guyana an ape-man specimen he named "Nondescript," consisting of the head and shoulders of a howler monkey with reshaped, humanlike facial features. Waterton's obvious hoax may have inspired Doyle's ape-men of *The Lost World*. The Guyanese "Nondescript" may have also inspired the unknown perpetrator of the Piltdown Man forgery (Winslow and Meyer 1983). As a source of primordial and counterfeit marvels, Guyana has provided a fascinating historical background to civilized men's search for human origins.

Doyle's novel later served as a basis for the movie *King Kong* (Pearsall 1977:131), in which the white woman is substituted for the Indian virgin to be sacrificed to the sexual appetite of the jungle beast. It is the white man's task to save the white woman, civilization, and himself from the beast within. King Kong offers a contest between civilized man and the savage. Victorious, the civilized man kills the beast, secures the white woman as his own, and acquires the beast's prerogatives in the previously forbidden domain of the primitive, tropical world.

The theme of the lost world is also transformed from a secret place where vulnerable and enticing virgins dwell to a self-contained world of women. Walter E. Roth, for many years a scholar of Guyana's indigenous peoples, recorded a tale of Amazons who are considerably more accommodating than their murderous counterparts of earlier versions. A party of men, led by an old man, approaches the interior world of Amazons governed by an old woman. She announces:

"All those who pass this way have to remain at least a year with us before we allow them to proceed on their journey. We will do our best to make you happy while you stay. Both you, old man, and every one of your companions must take two or three of our women to wife. At the end of the year, those of you who become fathers of girls are free to go your way, but those to whom boys are born must stay with us from year to year until you beget girls. You now know what is expected of you." (quoted in Roth 1915:222)

These women, who do not need men in their everyday lives, are forced to treat them as guests for the purpose of procreation. Men are admitted to this private female world for the women's own good. By the date of this version of the subdued Amazon, the presence of British government bureaucracy in the Guyanese interior was well established.

Alert to the stories of lost Amazons in the forest, anthropologist William C. Farabee (1918:166–167), who surveyed the Indians of Guyana's interior, made special mention of ten Wapishana women who lived in a female society. Having survived their husbands, these elderly widows had moved to a secluded hillock where they built a large communal house and cooperatively farmed. This world was comprised of aging Amazons.

In these perceptions, women are aloof with a parallel existence to that of men. Somehow men must break through time and space to subjective interiors where the dependent, childlike woman is waiting in a paradise for him. These psychological dramas were staged in Guyana's rain forests, which were increasingly pacified under British colonial rule. As the forests were settled and their resources developed, the Romance of the Wild Woman was preserved in the psychology of men.[7]

English novelist D. H. Lawrence (1917:125–136) expresses rapture in discovering a new world in his poem, "New Heaven and Earth":

> My God, but I can only say
> I touch, I feel the unknown!
> I am the first comer!

Cortes, Pisarro, Columbus, Cabot, they are nothing, nothing!
I am the first comer!
I am the discoverer!
I have found the other world!

The unknown, the unknown!
I am thrown upon the shore.
I am covering myself with the sand.
I am filling my mouth with the earth.
I am burrowing my body into the soil.
The unknown, the new world!
(Lawrence 1917:131–132, part 6, lines 21–34)

The man here speaks with the egoism of a child, unaware of the existence of others, in a world in which the self is paramount and any fantasy of self-importance is possible. It is an ancient world hidden in the psychological development of the individual. It is a world men try to recapture in unexplored lands and the bodies of women.

An Encounter with Giggling Women. After his divorce, novelist Evelyn Waugh visited a Benedictine commune in the Brazilian frontier town of Boa Vista, adjacent to Guyana. "Already in the few hours of my sojourn there," Waugh (1934a:120) wrote, "the Boa Vista of my imagination had come to grief." Waugh's disillusionment with this New World utopia accompanied his disappointment with the Indian women he encountered during a trip through the Guyanese interior.

Despite his expectations of an exotic paradise with provocative and willing nymphs, Waugh portrayed a reality of stubborn women. The distance between assumptions and actuality grows, as Waugh recorded in his diary a repartee with his black male guide, Haynes: "Pretty Indian girl named Rosa. Haynes flirtatious in old-womanly way. Said I could sleep with her but hedged when I tried to bring him to point" (1976:365). Elsewhere, the women Waugh met in the interior only "giggled" at him (1976:373–374). Waugh was inspired to create disparaging portrayals: One woman is "stocky and drab with a very sweet, child-like face"; another is "slatternly and ill-favored even for one of her race, with gross bandy legs, filthy and ragged clothes" (Waugh 1934a:180, 212).

Waugh subsequently wrote the novel *A Handful of Dust* (1934b) in which the final scenes take place in the jungle of Guyana. The hero, a divorced man, accompanies Dr. Messinger, who is seeking the legendary city of wonders in the deep interior. Their Indian guides are led by a passive, repulsive-looking woman who is asked to venture further into the bush:

> Rosa said nothing; her face was perfectly blank . . . the shadow of her high cheek bones hid her eyes; lank, ragged hair, a tenuous straggle of tattooing along forehead and lip, rotund body in its filthy cotton gown, bandy brown legs. (Waugh 1934b:257–258)

The Indians steal away, and Dr. Messinger drowns in a blossom-strewn pool. Fitful with fever, the hero stumbles on in his quest for utopia. Awakening later in the company of a recluse, the hero babbles about his elusive ex-wife, who is in love with a working-class man, and another business-minded woman who has converted paradise into flats with separate bathrooms for rent—"Very suitable for base love" (Waugh 1934b:288).

Waugh, like Hudson before him, contrasted the English woman with the Indian maid of Guyana. However, Waugh realized that the women of his expectations—the virgin as well as the Amazon—were illusions. Consequently, he portrayed all women as disappointing agents of male needs. Having made his way to the reputed location of worldly pleasure, Waugh's hero has no helpmate. Rather, he is condemned to reading Dickens's novels to an illiterate noble savage, the mad man who saved his life for this very purpose.

A Primitive Saturnalia. In his novelistic travelogue about the Guyanese interior, William J. LaVarre (1935:276) discovered a manless "Blight" that afflicted women who inhabited "a massively primeval country." More than a hundred Indian women are ostracized in an encampment because "they could apparently give birth only to female children" (La Varre 1935:277–278). The women, who hunt and fish for themselves, are economically independent and have their own political organization. Nevertheless, La Varre (1935:278) described this female community as "a place seething with man-hunger." These women desire sons so they may reenter the mixed society of men and women. With male guides and baggage carriers, these modern Amazons satiate their lusts by turning a "glamorous night into a primitive Saturnalia" (La Varre 1935:282). Unlike the treacherous Amazons of earlier lore, these women come to desire the men who subjugate them sexually. Thus, the subdued Amazon learns to enjoy her role as victim.

Similarly, in his book *The Barama River Caribs of British Guiana*, anthropologist John Gillin (1936) referred to a primitive world based on male dreams of conquering the woman who begs for fulfillment. Valued for their sexual youth, women in Gillin's analysis compete among each other to present themselves to the man who evaluates and sexually appropriates them. Gillin (1936:119–120) described the sexual dynamics of a Carib Indian household:

> Concerning the personalities of the three women in Miller's household, then, we see that Elizabeth is nominal head of the female side of household affairs. She, however, is greatly influenced in practical matters by the advice of Mary, whose greater age and experience she respects, while at the same time she has no reason to feel antagonism toward Mary as a sexual rival. Mary is nominally in the secondary position of rank and authority, but . . . is able to exert the strongest personal influence of all the three women in matters which are not involved with Miller's sexual feelings. Charlotte nominally is the subordinate one of the three women, but, due to her apparently increasing hold on the affections of Miller, is gradually gaining more and more actual importance in the household. She is now well on the way to being a serious rival of Elizabeth as nominal mistress of the household. All of this is not to say, however, that the rivalry between the women of this polygamous household has as yet, at least, reached the point of open hostilities.

Gillin assumed that sexual rivalry jeopardizes cooperation

among co-wives. In his estimation, Mary, "toothless and wrinkled, with black hair streaming about her leathery shoulders and flap-like breasts," is marginal because she is old (Gillin 1936:101). To delay the same fate, Elizabeth, "young, buxom, well rounded, and smooth-skinned," must hold her position against the sexual charms of a younger woman (Gillin 1936:101). Actually, Carib social structure reveals important relations of solidarity among women, who usually select their own co-wives (Adams 1978, 1981, n.d.). In Gillin's account, women fight each other for men's sexual favors—an inversion of the Amazon's war against men.

Nicholas Guppy (1958:103) came upon "the most beautiful Indian woman [he] had ever seen" during his travels along the Guyanese-Brazilian border to record the habits of the Wai-Wai Indians there. She was "about sixteen, with a turned-up nose, down which she had painted a line of red paint" (Guppy 1958:103–104). She had "plump, erect breasts, a smooth, firm, belly, well-shaped hips, and legs which met all the way down to her toes when she stood with them together" (Guppy 1958:104). She wore nothing but a pubic "apron of red cloth, earrings, and a necklace . . . with a large safety-pin hanging in the middle where a civilized girl might have a crucifix" (Guppy 1958:104). Described as "a sort of Wai-Wai Lollobrigida" (Guppy 1958:104), this young Indian wife presented a tableau for the seven men she accompanied on a canoe trip up river.

Sexual motives may also be assigned to Indian women of the interior. In a chronicle of calamities in modern men's search for El Dorado, writer Victor G. C. Norwood (1960:34) described one of the "dusky courtesans" who was "whoring her way from one camp to another." Like the sixteenth-century image of the vulnerable Indian maid, Norwood's demimondaine travels alone or in the company of gold and diamond prospectors. Mute and partially naked, she has repulsive bare feet with "deep cracks and broken nails" and wears a "thin, ragged cotton frock" that emphasizes her pregnant condition (Norwood 1960:34). The virgin promise of bountifulness is in this case an exaggeration of pregnancy, which confirms the status of the "fallen" woman. In this modern version of the exotic New World maiden, the Wild Woman who promises sexual submission evokes revulsion.

Journalist Colin Henfrey (1965) rehearsed another variation of the Wild Woman by portraying Guyanese Indian women in terms of their personal sexual histories. Illicit experience becomes a stigma which adds to their appeal as inhabitants of a demimonde. School teacher Carlita loses her job because she has an illegitimate child. Henfrey (1965:71) meets this "belle of the village" at a party:

> There was something defiant in her figure, barefoot, in a pale green dress. I got up and danced with her. I could feel the weight of her jet-black hair, tumbling carelessly over her shoulders and reaching down almost to her waist. Once or twice she looked up shyly. Somehow, like all the others around us, she was still wild and free.

In this case, a naive woman is victim of her uncontrolled sexual appetite, a heritage of her Amazon/Indian background. Carlita represents the Romance of the Wild Woman as a "fallen" woman who nonetheless gratifies men's sexual egos. Her very existence, which is exciting yet unacceptable, validates images of the punished woman that serve the collective fantasies of men. Carlita, like her "fallen" Victorian counterpart, is created by male imaginations and sexual acts. Sentimentalized by men, she is eventually discarded by them.[8]

The Mother-Monster

In Guyanese novelist Edgar Mittelholzer's *Corentyne Thunder* (1941), an East Indian, Sosee, made motherhood a sinecure by bearing seven children for a white planter: "For her he felt apathy, or disgust, or anger" (Mittelholzer [1941] 1970:40). Yet the planter had seen the nubile Sosee in a different way: "a healthy female slave whom he had brought into his house to satisfy his sexual needs and to reproduce his kind" (Mittelholzer [1941] 1970:94).

The planter selects their eldest son Geoffry to be his reincarnation and delights in Geoffry's exploits. On his school vacation, Geoffry is rejected by Sosee's younger half-sister. In contrast to Sosee, this sister is seductive: "The dark points of her breasts seemed like eyes of mystery" (Mittelholzer [1941] 1970:200). Geoffry has an (incestuous) affair with Sosee's second, even younger, sister. He intends to take no responsibility for her pregnancy, which would interfere with his future in England. By rejecting his child borne by his mother's sister—a social replication of the union that produced him—Geoffry in a sense rejects himself. The sexuality of Guyanese women is the agent and their motherhood the cause of alienation among Anglophile Guyanese men.

This aversion to motherhood continues in contemporary anthropology about Guyana. Raymond T. Smith's influential book, *The Negro Family in British Guiana* (1956), defined a mother-dominated family. Casual sexual liaisons characterize the first stage of the domestic cycle that Smith identified. In the second stage, a household is established by a conjugal pair, and the woman and children are dependent on the husband/father. As the children grow and enter the labor market, the mother acquires greater economic independence, which includes a lien on her children's incomes. Her daughters may bring illegitimate children into the household, thereby extending the senior woman's mothering role as her own reproductive career ends. In this third stage, the mother has as much earning capacity as the father. However, she continues to control the activities of her daughters' children, while the status of the husband/father declines (R. T. Smith 1956:70).

A man's earning capacity remains more or less constant throughout his career, despite irregular employment (R. T. Smith 1956:46). In that case, as his economic position in the labor force neither deteriorates nor improves, how is the husband/father's status overshadowed in his own household? The answer, according to Smith (1956:143), lies in the cultural value placed on the mother-child bond, which promotes a coalition of the mother and adult children against the husband/father. Thus, a seesaw relation emerges between a woman and a man opposed by the fulcrum of marriage. At first the male sexually pursues and exploits the young woman. As this stage is replaced by consensual or legal marriage, male dominance is eventually eclipsed by the growing family command of the mother/wife. Having first encountered the virgin, the man is eventually co-opted in his own home by the domineering mother into whom the virgin has metamorphosed.

The unwritten but logically implied addendum to Smith's interpretation is that Western men, unlike the Afro-Guyanese, can secure their patriarchal families and their privileges with women through economic and sexual superiority. Smith's study also carries a warning of women's fate without masterful men. Although manless women build personal domains as mothers, they remain isolated from the larger society. This study of the mother-dominated family is an object lesson for Westerners, while its impact in Guyana is to intensify the sexual definition of women among the Afro-Guyanese. Such scholarship invites false assumptions about a natural hierarchy prevailing between women and men.

After some four hundred years of subordination, native populations named "Indians" by Columbus have accommodated to the views that outsiders hold of them. Men exaggerate their fierceness, and women demonstrate their alternate virgin/Amazon status. For example, anthropologist Audrey Butt (1957) described the facial tattoos applied to Akawaio Indian women as they anticipate motherhood. Scorpions, stinging bees, and anaconda snakes decorate the mouths of Akawaio mothers, an obvious allusion to *vagina dentata*, the sexually consuming mouth. The facial tattooing exhibits the image of women as man-eaters. Within the context of an imposed ideology regarding what Indians are supposed to be like, these Amazon-like masks announce their wearers as subservient people who mimic exploitative self-images in order to survive.

Woman as virgin/Amazon also occurs in contemporary Indian myths. Several collected by anthropologist Lee Drummond (1977) portray the relation between man as hunter and woman as prey. In a version recorded among the Arawaks of the Pomeroon River region of Guyana, a "white bitch" is transformed into a woman and performs domestic chores while the master is not watching. The man keeps his pet wife by destroying the dog's skin out of which she has stepped. Similarly, in a Guyanese Carib version, a howler monkey carcass changes into a beautiful virgin whom the hunter makes his dutiful wife. However, these fantastic wives can revert into wild animals, especially when they become mothers. The Guyanese Caribs also tell a story about a foreboding world of women who tie up a man as they would a pet monkey. They decide to kill him because he tries to conquer them with sex. These Guyanese Indian stories repeat themes expressed by outsiders since the sixteenth century.

The Guyanese novelist Wilson Harris substituted an aged woman for a virgin in *Palace of the Peacock* (1968). An Indian grandmother seductively appears to a group of men seeking their fortunes on a boat trip into the interior:

> Tiny embroideries resembling the handwork on the Arawak woman's kerchief and the wrinkles on her brow turned to incredible and fast soundless breakers of foam. Her crumpled bosom and river grew agitated with desire, bottling and shaking every fear and inhibition and outcry. The ruffles in the water were her dress rolling and rising to embrace the crew. This sudden insolence of soul rose and caught them from the powder of her eyes and the age of her smile and the dust in her hair all flowing back upon them with silent streaming majesty and abnormal youth and in a wave of freedom and strength. (W. Harris 1968:73)

The historical legacy of the New World as virgin/Amazon is changed. Guyana, especially the rain forest interior, is portrayed in Harris's novel as an ancient crone. Silent and alluring, the virgin/Amazon survives all her encounters with men, who are led to their deaths.

In this version, the terrible Amazon presents herself as a harmless old woman—all that is left for Guyanese nationals who seek to build their own bases of power through personal conquest. The decrepit woman contains in her past the virgin whom modern Guyanese, like earlier conquistadors, long to possess. Rather then escaping the Western, projective imagination of Guyana as woman, the image is refitted to serve the psychological and cultural expectations of men in their exploits against women and the less powerful (Adams 1982).

Novelist Shiva Naipaul (1983:1) explores defeat and despair in post-colonial Cuyama, a thinly disguised Guyana, "a tract of land on the fringe of an Empire whose interests had always laid elsewhere." Dina St Pierre is a main character in this "sun-stunned vacuum separating ocean from jungle" (S. Naipaul 1983:5). Like Cuyama—"this sterile patch of earth perched on the edge of a cruel continent" (S. Naipaul 1983:63)—Dina is a zero. She is a modern woman with East Indian and Portuguese heritages which she has shed: "She was formless, lacking a geometry; concocted out of a primal dust upon which no god had ever stamped its imprint" (S. Naipaul 1983:105).

The indolent Dina reads D. H. Lawrence to pass the time and stands aloof from her bewildered husband and alienated child. Pushed into a responsive role, Naipaul's Dina offers vacuity, like the empty "hot country" she despises. In this harsh and unsympathetic novel, Naipaul interprets the historic theme of creating new lives in a utopian New World setting. In his version of a New World void, Naipaul rehearses once again relations of sex and submission between men and women.

Creating images of women in Guyana have been men's exercises in definition without the benefit of dialogue for five centuries. Taking form in men's projective imaginations, women—who are nothing in themselves—must be conquered. Women are to perform what men expect in regard to their egoistic demands, and women are penalized for disappointing men's fantastic expectations which cannot possibly be fulfilled.

The Romance of the Wild Woman is more than a personal projection in the intimate relations men have with women. The romance articulated in the Guyana as woman metaphor is adjusted to the historical circumstances of conquest and yet persistently conveys vested political interests. The underdeveloped world understood as a woman and woman understood as the underdeveloped world justify and reinforce each other as negations. This ideological system invites men to exploit women and underdeveloped worlds that translate into each other. After conquering these worlds for their own, men find them dull. Worlds under submission no longer evoke men's sexual and egoistic attention. However, resistance in any form renders the woman of other worlds into the monster-Amazon, whom nature has hidden within the deepest recesses of unexplored terrain. Resistance provokes the rage of the huntsman who, according to these formulas, assumes that the woman is begging to be conquered.

This ideological system presents for men a no-lose gambit. Women who try to please men are ravaged and abandoned; women who fight are seeking destruction. Explorers, soldiers of fortune, and, more recently, agents of economic change in the Third World have had their interests served by these mythological fantasies of woman/America/Guyana-as-virgin/Amazon. Scholars, novelists, and travelers have repeated these fantasies, which involve men in a collective advantage, and in which self-accomplishment is confused with the destruction of women. The mythological system that emerges ruthlessly denies human status to women or to others who are less powerful. With such elaborations in Western ideas and literature, every man as hunter can self-righteously face any less powerful adversary as woman.

5. The Romance Revisited

> A woman is an important thing. A man is a
> worthless thing indeed, because a woman gives
> birth to the people of the country. What work
> can a man do? A woman bears a child, then takes
> a hoe, goes to the field, and is working there;
> she feeds the child (with the work) there.[1]
>
> Nsaw women of West Central Africa, 1952

Women are experts on their lives. The absence of their testimony has impoverished anthropology. Indeed, the few times that their voices have emerged reveal a complexity that the Romance of the Wild Woman cannot encompass.

Women's narratives, such as those collected by Lurie (1961), Shostak (1981), M. F. Smith (1955), and Kaberry (1952), document the diversity of women's experiences. Women are in the center of historical forces; and women create culture. The wealth of this small literature enriches our understanding of the human condition. Mountain Wolf Woman, Nisa, and Baba—the women whose testimonies are cited above, including the women quoted at the beginning of this chapter—would not recognize themselves as forms of the Wild Woman.

Men invented the Wild Woman, and in their romance with her, perpetuate male supremacy. In this mythic process, the Wild Woman holds up a mirror that reveals the selves men desire to be. As yet, the small literature about women's lives has done little to redress this pervasive exercise of male power.

The dream world about women in exotic other worlds, where the imagined comes true, is seen through men's eyes. Men use remote places as playgrounds for their psyches. They enjoy experiences in a reality they have created far from home, while women in these male-defined worlds are rendered silent and passive.

Images of woman in this and other worlds obscure for men what they have created for their own satisfactions. Woman exists in deference to the male ego, which is privy to bring unexamined, self-indulgent demands to social relations. Documented in natural history, anthropology, biology, and repeated in literature, woman's role in nature is to inspire and then submit to judgment. *Émile,* Jean Jacques Rousseau's ([1762] 1911:325) influential work on education, emphasized this understanding of woman's purpose:

> To be pleasing in his sight, to win his respect and love, to train him in childhood, to tend him in manhood, to counsel and console, to make his life pleasant and happy, these are the duties of woman for all time, and this is what she should be taught while she is young.

Every woman must endure men's rightful scrutiny of her sexual appeal and behavior. In colleagueship with his readers—presumably male—Rousseau sketched the image of woman they collectively possess as a private fantasy of power.

In response to Rousseau's *Émile,* feminist Mary Wollstonecraft wrote *A Vindication of the Rights of Woman* ([1792] 1975). Wollstonecraft critically examined the prejudices that served to exclude women from education in order to make them the obedient objects of men's desires. She wryly commented: "Tyrants and sensualists are in the right when they endeavour to keep women in the dark, because the former only want slaves, and the latter a play-thing" (Wollstonecraft [1792] 1975:24). Wollstonecraft recognized that women can be pets or servants—roles that imprison the body and the mind.

Men view themselves in terms of what others are not. According to feminist Andrea Dworkin (1976:11), "The male sexual model is based on a polarization of humankind into man/woman, master/slave, aggressor/victim, active/passive." This asymmetry emphasizes the chasm of inequality between men and women, and the violence against women that is vital for men's identities.

Men who enter the world of women or the underdeveloped world leave behind the codes that relate men to other men. Travel to these other worlds erotically stirs men's senses as the male self meets the savage unrestraint of the female other. The male ego matches itself with the Wild Woman who is thought to have furtive sources of power, particularly sexual power conceived in men's terms of the castrating Amazon, who conquers and kills the hapless male intruder. As anthropologist Elsie Clews Parsons (1913:273) explained, "A dangerous woman makes a brave man." The male observer creates the feminized other, who is thought to be a part of nature in exotic nether worlds.

Themes in the imagination of exotic worlds include the desire to see women naked and victimized. Men enjoy their conquests in staged paradises and transfer their self-proclaimed prerogatives as rulers to their own societies. What is done to the Wild Woman in savage lands is in store for the woman in the civilized world should she misinterpret her place. The Romance of the Wild Woman in the tropics simultaneously serves to reinforce the imprisonment of women within civilization. The image keepers of all women are civilized men.

FEMALE TERRAIN

The idea of woman as a state of potential is only possible in relation to the aggression of men. Likewise, patriarchy is supposed to have resulted from the overthrow of matriarchy in the march of civilization. As men come to dominate women in the course of cultural evolution, the world of women is seen as a lost world—a world left behind, a relic of earlier, primitive stages of savagery and barbarism. Today, women of the Third World afford men a quick trip back to the beginnings. On this primeval stage, modern men act as conquistadors.

The woman who resists conquest is the Amazon. She destroys rather than procreates in the sexual act. The Amazon devours men instead of submitting to a passive role. Yet men assume that this Wild Woman really wants to be conquered and that she will love the man who subdues her. Invested with demonic qualities, the Amazon waits for the man who attempts this test and fails.

Using the metaphor of sex and conquest, men enter the wilderness, a vast emptiness whose only purpose is to exist for them. Feminist Angela Carter (1978:4) identified this "elementary iconography" of woman: "Between her legs lies nothing but zero, the sign for nothing, that only becomes something when the male principle fills it with meaning." But it is a meaning over which men seek to maintain private ownership. Woman makes this meaning possible, but she does not participate in it.

Because women do not remain eternal virgins with endless potential, men find them revolting. Disenchanted during his trip to the deflowered New World, anthropologist Claude Lévi-Strauss (1961:99) commented:

> In the outskirts of São Paulo, as later in the State of New York, in Connecticut, and even in the Rocky Mountains, I became familiar with a Nature which, though more savage than our own, because less populated and less under cultivation, had yet lost all its original freshness: Nature not so much "wild" as degraded.

This canvas of invidious contrasts has been a disservice to anthropology, the societies observed, and the women within them. Nature, woman, and the wilderness resonate men's disappointing fantasies. Men's dream world of the matriarch, the virgin, and the Amazon insinuates powerful cultural forces that penalize all women.

PERSON AS WOMAN

Knowledge is power to maintain privilege. Knowledge is also power to criticize and to change. Learning to know ourselves as women requires demystifying the past. At times it requires the painful process of discarding male-defined knowledge. It is difficult for us to shift from the passive to an active state of mind, language, and social relations, given the pervasiveness of ideas like the Wild Woman.

The quest for self begins by recognizing that woman is a derived construct based on male interests obscured in romance. Mastering the Wild Woman in exotic worlds of conquest and colonialism, as well as subjugating the Wild Woman who lurks in all civilized women, is a cultural imperative of Western, male thinking.

Woman as body becomes an object detached from mind whose attributes are determined by what men choose to recognize. The psychic and social consequences for womanhood are evident. The Wild Woman is eroticized as a sexual pet; the woman with a mind is derogated as having a sexless body. Woman can have mind or body, but not both; either option results in psychic and social crippling.

The Romance of the Wild Woman achieved elaborate geographical expression in the male imagination: the New World, an untapped cornucopia of riches for the taking; the Dark Continent, sullen and brutal, yielding its riches grudgingly; the South Seas, a Garden of Eden. The remote Wild Woman, like unexplored terrain, is both the beauty and the beast. She promises fulfillment but offers disappointment. Literature about exotic lands, including anthropology, is filled with litanies of disillusionment in the quest for riches or knowledge.

The Wild Woman is body incarnate, and the world she inhabits is the playground where men act out their fantasies and pursue their indulgences. Men return from these nether worlds enriched and experienced. The quest for the Wild Woman in foreign lands is the white man's rite of passage into maturity.

Anthropology reinforces and legitimizes this romance. Returning alive from fieldwork quests, anthropologists establish themselves as professional interpreters of the bodies and habits of indigenous others. Anthropologists thus become the self-taught experts on the Wild Woman.

The Wild Woman communicates multiple meanings swinging from the sentimentalized mother-martyr to the opposite pole of man-eating Amazon. In partial undress, the Wild Woman promises sexual delights, which can be taken by brute force if necessary. In contrast, the crone with betel-stained teeth and sagging breasts, as well as the evil-minded temptress described in literary and anthropological genres, invites contempt. Most important, the Wild Woman evokes terror of the unknown. She arouses apprehension by her secret knowledge and by her power to act upon it. The Wild Woman may behave naively from an outsider's point of view, but there is always the chance of a deadly scheme that is more than mere trickery or conniving. The Wild Woman can create; she can also subvert and destroy. CopperWoman

We cannot combat that which is nameless. Once we articulate those ideas and their dynamics that hold women prisoners, we can confront them. The Romance of the Wild Woman is a constellation of ideas, images, and motives set against the stark contrast of what the ideal woman should be. Recognizing the Romance of the Wild Woman as alienation of mind and body for all women is a critical step toward rejecting definitions of ourselves in male eyes. Men have sought self-enrichment by using women's backs, brains, and wombs. Understanding historical and contemporary versions of the Romance of the Wild Woman enables us to resist this co-optation and to take up the challenge of creating new realities.

Notes

1. THE ARCHAIC MATRIARCH

1. Adrienne Rich, "Foreword. Conditions for Work: The Common World of Women," in *Working It Out: Twenty-Three Women Writers, Artists, Scientists, and Scholars Talk about Their Lives and Work,* eds. Sara Ruddick and Pamela Daniels (New York: Random House, Pantheon Books, 1977), p. xv.

2. Suggested sources on the history of political and philosophical ideas about women include: Agonito (1977); Clark and Lange (1979); Coward (1983); Eisenstein (1981); Elshtain (1981); Jaggar (1983); McMillan (1982); Merchant (1980); M. Obrien (1981); Okin (1979); and Whitbeck (1976).

For discussions of the women/culture/nature problem see: Guillaumin (1981); MacCormack and Strathern (1980); Mathieu (1978, 1980); and Ortner (1974).

Works that influenced our thinking about images of women include: Bernheimer (1952); Cohn (1975); Dudley and Novak (1972); Taylor (1979); and Warner (1981).

3. Sources on women and the sociology of knowledge include Glennon (1979), Harding and Hintikka (1983), Sherman and Beck (1979), and Tiffany (n.d.a). For an introduction to the rapidly growing anthropological literature about women, see Tiffany (1982c). Detailed review essays on recent anthropological publications appear occasionally in *Signs: Journal of Women in Culture and Society.* The following works illustrate the diversity of anthropological approaches to feminist issues: Leacock (1981, 1983a, 1983b); Martin and Voorhies (1975); Ortner and Whitehead (1981); Quinn (1977); Reiter (1975); Rogers (1978); Rosaldo (1974, 1980, 1983); Sacks (1979); Sanday (1981); Schlegel (1977); M. Strathern (1980, 1981, 1984); and Tiffany (1978, 1979a, 1982b, n.d.b., n.d.d).

103

4. During the 1920s, R. S. Rattray, barrister-at-law and captain of the Gold Coast Political Service, commented on the disenfranchisement of senior women in ruling clans in Ashanti society: "To-day the Queen Mothers are unrecognized by us [British colonial administration] and their position and influence are rapidly passing away" (Rattray 1923:84). Anthropologist Judith Van Allen (1972) documented this dual process of silencing women and rendering them powerless during British rule in Africa.

5. Literature on the anthropology of fieldwork rarely addresses the issues raised here from a feminist perspective. For further discussion see Gonzalez (1984), D. O'Brien (1984), Poewe (1982), Scheper-Hughes (1983), and Tiffany (1984, n.d.a, n.d.c).

6. Awareness of the relation between researcher and informant is explored in diverse ways. See J. Freeman (1979), Golde (1970), Nachman (1983), Ruby (1982), Scholte (1972), and A. Strathern (1979).

7. Duffin (1978), Eichler (1980), Fausto-Sterling (1981), Fee (1976, 1980), Lowe and Hubbard (1983), Mosedale (1978), and Stark-Adamec (1981) discuss issues of feminism and scientific inquiry.

8. Our purpose here is to consider the persistence of matriarchal ideas, rather than to marshall evidence to confirm or refute the social reality of matriarchy. For additional reading on anthropological perspectives about matriarchy, "mother right," and female power see: Bamberger (1974); Barstow (1978); Fluehr-Lobban (1979); Leacock (1972); Poewe (1981); Rohrlich (1980); Sacks (1974); Tiffany (1982a); and Webster (1975).

9. Frederick Engels's classic work, *The Origin of the Family, Private Property, and the State* (1884), borrowed heavily from the study of Iroquois society published by Lewis Henry Morgan (1877), an American attorney who assisted the Iroquois of New York State with land claims. Iroquois relations of production and reproduction illustrated Engels's savage stage of human development. Iroquois women exercised considerable economic and political power prior to intensive Western contact (see Brown 1970, Grumet 1980, and Shimony 1980).

10. Sources that shaped our understanding of Victorian women and society, in addition to those cited in the text, include: Best (1971); Delamont and Duffin (1978); Hill (1980); Houghton (1957); Lane (1980); Murray (1982); Pichanick (1980); B. Smith (1981);

Vicinus (1972b, 1977); Walkowitz (1980); Welter (1966a); and Winkler (1980).

11. Branca (1975:121–127), Bullough (1976:530–563), Cott (1978), Degler (1974), Foucault (1978), Gay (1984), Mosedale (1978), Rosenberg (1973), F. B. Smith (1977), and Weeks (1981) discuss Victorian ideas about female sexuality.

The growing literature on gender differences in perception and behavior emphasizes the importance of female worlds and the diversity of women's supportive relationships, including female friendships. See, for example, Bernard (1981), Cott (1977), Faderman (1981), Kern (1981), Smith-Rosenberg (1975), and Ulrich (1982).

Recent works that consider women in biological and evolutionary perspective include: Bleier (1984); Hrdy (1981); Hubbard et al. (1982); Leibowitz (1983); Sayers (1982); Tanner (1981); and Zihlman (1981).

12. For further consideration of negative attitudes in which cultural aspects of the menstrual cycle are discussed, see Harrell (1981) and Meigs (1976).

2. ENCOUNTERS WITH THE WILD WOMAN

1. Joseph Conrad, *Heart of Darkness*, 2nd rev. ed. by Robert Kimbrough (1899; reprint, New York: Norton, 1971), p. 35.

2. Sources that influenced our thinking about the Romance of the Wild Woman, in addition to those cited in the text, include: Albers and Medicine (1983); Boutilier (1984); Campbell (1980); Curti (1980); Curtin (1964); Dally (1982); Dworkin (1981); Etienne and Leacock (1980); Fairchild (1928); Foucault (1972); Glacken (1967); P. Grimshaw (1983); Inglis (1974); Kolodny (1984); Lowe (1982); and D. O'Brien (n.d.).

3. A list of reviews, including newspaper, magazine, and journal articles about Freeman's book would fill several pages. Readers interested in anthropologists' reactions to the debate may consult volume 85 of the December 1983 issue of the *American Anthropologist*, which presented a special section on Freeman's book. For other views on the Freeman-Mead controversy see Elshtain (1983) and Nardi (1984).

4. For anthropological examples of these sexualized contrasts, see: Chagnon (1983 [discussed in chapter 3]); Dumont (1978:42, 64);

M. Harris (1974:83–107; 1977:45–54); and Siskind (1973a). For similar examples in fiction see: Conrad (1899); Llosa (1968); Melville (1846); S. Naipaul (1983 [discussed in chapter 4]); Ribeiro (1984); Souza (1977); Stevenson (1904); and Waugh (1934b [discussed in chapter 4]).

5. Sources that shaped our understanding of the Wild Woman in fiction include: Beer (1974); Fetterley (1983); Gardner (1977); Gilbert and Gubar (1979); Herzog (1983); Kolodny (1975); Laracy and Laracy (1977); Martin (1971); Modleski (1982); D. O'Brien (n.d.); Saxton (1977); Street (1975); and Watt (1979).

Anthropologists have used literary genres as sources for the concepts they provide. In her classic work, *Patterns of Culture* (1934), anthropologist Ruth Benedict described Apollonian and Dionysian themes in Native American cultures. Like the linguist Edward Sapir, Benedict was also a poet (Handler 1983; Modell 1983).

6. Translations of indigenous words used in Malinowski's diary were taken from the index included in the back of the book.

7. Many writers who use anthropological materials for a general audience convey misogynistic views about women. For example: Ardrey (1966, 1970); Goldberg (1974); M. Harris (1972, 1974); Morris (1967); Tiger (1969); Tiger and Fox (1971), and Wilson (1978).

3. THE PRIMITIVE WOMAN

1. Eric R. Wolf, *Anthropology* (Englewood Cliffs, New Jersey: Prentice-Hall, 1964), p. 12.

2. See Asad (1973), Douglas (1980), Johnson (1979), and Kuper (1973) for discussions of Evans-Pritchard and British social anthropology in colonial Africa.

3. Patrilineal (or agnatic) descent refers to ancestry reckoned exclusively through the paternal (male) line. Kinship groups in Nuer society are organized as patrilineages (patrilineal descent groups). Members of a patrilineage reckon their descent from a common male ancestor through known genealogical links traced through the paternal line. Children in patrilineal descent systems, then, are members of their father's patrilineage. See also Evans-Pritchard (1950:38–40).

4. A lineage is a kinship-based group whose members reckon descent, either matrilineally (through females) or patrilineally (through males), from a common ancestor through demonstrated genealogical links. Lineages are commonly referred to as unilineal

descent groups in the anthropological literature. A clan is a kinship group consisting of a number of lineages whose members believe they are descendants of a common ancestor, even though they may not be able to demonstrate exact genealogical relationships.

5. Bridewealth, or brideprice, refers to the transfer of valuables by the groom and/or his kin to the bride's relatives.

7. Bohannan (1963:77–80) and Lewis (1976:249–259) illustrate traditional concern with the priority of men's legal claims, whereas, Feil (1981) and Ogbu (1978) criticize anthropological emphasis on male rights in the study of marriage systems.

7. A leviratic union occurs when a man marries his deceased brother's widow (or demands bridewealth from another man she marries) and has an obligation to provide for her. The term comes from the Latin *levir*, brother-in-law. Ghost marriage refers to the ceremonial marriage of a woman to the name of a male relative who died without male children. In woman-marriage, a woman gives bridewealth for and marries another woman, thus acquiring rights over the latter and her children (see Krige 1974, Oboler 1980, and D. O'Brien 1977). For additional discussion of these forms of marriage in Nuer society, see Evans-Pritchard (1938).

8. Elizabeth Salter's (1971) biography of Daisy Bates, who spent much of her long life living and working among Australian aborigines, is a fascinating portrait of a complex Victorian woman. Academic anthropologists ignored Bates's work, which was hampered by lack of funding. Salter (1971:152–153, 176) suggests that Bates's research findings were plagiarized by the young A. R. Radcliffe-Brown, whose career in anthropology was firmly established by his publications on Australian aboriginal social organization. Anthropologist Rodney Needham (1974) supports Salter's contention. For an opposing view on this issue see I. White (1981).

9. Hart worked among the Tiwi during 1928 and 1929, Pilling during 1953 and 1954, and Goodale in 1954, 1962, and during 1980 and 1981. For further discussion on this issue see Tiffany (1984).

10. Recognizing that researchers often respond to the psychological and cultural expectations of their readers, anthropologists have questioned Chagnon's view of a warlike Yanomama (Chambers 1981; Davis 1976).

11. Readers interested in additional sources will find Ramos's (1979) and Shapiro's (1972, 1976) discussions of Yanomama society from a female perspective worthwhile. Helena Valero, a Spaniard,

lived for twenty years with the Yanomama, who captured her as a child. Her account is compelling reading (Biocca 1969). Tiffany (n.d.d.) provides a feminist interpretation of women's work and reproductive roles in Yanomama society.

12. For further discussion of the impact of these changes on the Yanomama, see Chagnon and Melacon (1983), Lizot (1976b), and Saffirio and Hames (1983).

4. THE VIRGIN AND THE AMAZON

1. This song was collected in 1971 by Kathleen J. Adams during her anthropological fieldwork with Carib Indians in Guyana. A grandmother sang it toward the end of an evening of drinking and singing.

2. John Locke, *The Second Treatise of Civil Government and a Letter Concerning Toleration*, ed. and introduction by John W. Gough (1690; reprint, Oxford: Basil Blackwell, 1946), p. 26.

3. Many references cited in this chapter have been published in numerous editions. We have used the earliest ones available to us. With readability in mind, the language of quoted passages from early works has been modernized.

4. Sources that stimulated our thinking about the New World, excluding those cited in the text, include: Baird (1982); Glacken (1967); Kandell (1984); Keen (1971); S. Naipaul (1981); V. S. Naipaul (1962, 1967, 1969); and Nash (1978).

5. Guyana, independent since 1966, has had several variants of its name, including Guiana and British Guiana. Except for titles or quotations from other works, the contemporary name is used.

6. For further discussion on the language of naming see LaBelle (1980), Leach (1964), Schulz (1975), and Spender (1980).

7. For discussion of the psychology of exploration and colonization, see: Baudet (1965); Kiernan (1969); Mannoni (1964); Marcuse (1955); and Nichols (1979–80).

8. Medicine (1983) discusses the pressure on Native American women to conform to "Indian-ness."

5. THE ROMANCE REVISITED

1. Phyllis M. Kaberry, *Women of the Grassfields: A Study of the Economic Position of Women in Bamenda, British Cameroons* (London: Her Majesty's Stationery Office, 1952), p. 150.

Bibliography

Adams, Kathleen J.
   1978   Barama River Carib Kinship: Brother-Brother and Mother-Daughter Identity Merging in a Two-Section System. In *Working Papers on South American Indians: Social Correlates of Kin Terminology, No. 1*, ed. David John Thomas, pp. 3–12. Bennington, Vermont: Bennington College.
   1981   The Role of Children in the Changing Socio-Economic Strategies of the Guyanese Caribs. *Canadian Journal of Anthropology* 2(1):61–66.
   1982   Gold, Utopia, and Guyana. In *Guyana Gold: The Story of Wellesley A. Baird, Guyana's Greatest Miner*, by Wellesley A. Baird, pp. 165–181. Washington, D.C.: Three Continents Press.
   n.d.   The Premise of Equality in Carib Societies. *Anthropologica*, in press.

Agonito, Rosemary
   1977   *History of Ideas on Woman: A Source Book.* New York: Putnam, Capricorn Books.

Albers, Patricia, and Beatrice Medicine, eds.
   1983   *The Hidden Half: Studies of Plains Indian Women.* Washington, D.C.: University Press of America.

Ardener, Edwin
   1972   Belief and the Problem of Women. In *The Interpretation of Ritual: Essays in Honour of A. I. Richards*, ed. J. S. La Fontaine, pp. 135–158. London: Tavistock Publications.

Ardrey, Robert
   1966   *The Territorial Imperative: A Personal Inquiry into the*

Animal Origins of Property and Nations. New York: Dell, Delta Books.
1970 *The Social Contract: A Personal Inquiry into the Evolutionary Sources of Order and Disorder.* New York: Atheneum.

Asad, Talal, ed.
1973 *Anthropology and the Colonial Encounter.* New York: Humanities Press.

Bachofen, Johann Jakob
1861 *Myth, Religion, and Mother Right: Selected Writings of J. J. Bachofen.* Translated by Ralph Manheim, preface by George Boas, and introduction by Joseph Campbell. Reprint. Princeton, New Jersey: Princeton University Press, Bollingen Series, no. 84, 1967.

Baird, Wellesley A.
1982 *Guyana Gold: The Story of Wellesley A. Baird, Guyana's Greatest Miner.* Washington, D.C.: Three Continents Press.

Bamberger, Joan
1974 The Myth of Matriarchy: Why Men Rule in Primitive Society. In *Woman, Culture, and Society,* eds. Michelle Zimbalist Rosaldo and Louise Lamphere, pp. 263–280. Stanford: Stanford University Press.

Barstow, Anne
1978 The Uses of Archeology for Women's History: James Mellaart's Work on the Neolithic Goddess at Çatal Hüyük. *Feminist Studies* 4(3):7–18.

Baudet, Henri
1965 *Paradise on Earth: Some Thoughts on European Images of Non-European Man.* Translated by Elizabeth Wentholt. Reprint. Westport, Connecticut: Greenwood Press, 1976.

Beard, Mary Ritter, ed.
1942 A Study of the *Encyclopedia Britannica* in Relation to Its Treatment of Women. In *Mary Ritter Beard: A Sourcebook,* ed. Ann J. Lane, pp. 215–224. Reprint. New York: Schocken Books, 1977.

Beattie, John
1964 *Other Cultures: Aims, Methods, and Achievements in Social Anthropology.* New York: Macmillan, Free Press.

Beebe, Charles W.
  1919   *Jungle Peace.* New York: H. Holt and Co.
Beer, Patricia
  1974   *Reader, I Married Him: A Study of the Women Characters of Jane Austen, Charlotte Brontë, Elizabeth Gaskell, and George Eliot.* New York: Harper & Row, Barnes and Noble.
Behn, Aphra
  1688   *Oroonoko; or, the History of the Royal Slave.* In *Shorter Novels: Seventeenth-Century,* ed. Philip Henderson, pp. 147–224. Reprint. London: J. M. Dent & Sons, 1930.
Benedict, Ruth
  1934   *Patterns of Culture.* Reprint. New York: New American Library of World Literature, Mentor Books, 1959.
Berkhofer, Robert F., Jr.
  1978   *The White Man's Indian: Images of the American Indian from Columbus to the Present.* New York: Random House, Vintage Books.
Bernard, Jessie
  1981   *The Female World.* New York: Macmillan, Free Press.
Bernheimer, Richard
  1952   *Wild Men in the Middle Ages: A Study in Art, Sentiment, and Demonology.* Reprint. New York: Farrar, Straus, & Giroux, Octagon Books, 1970.
Bernstein, Richard
  1983   Samoa: A Paradise Lost? *The New York Times Magazine* (24 April), section 6.
Best, Geoffrey
  1971   *Mid-Victorian Britain, 1851–1875.* New York: Schocken Books.
Billington, Ray Allen
  1981   *Land of Savagery, Land of Promise: The European Image of the American Frontier in the Nineteenth Century.* New York: Norton.
Biocca, Ettore
  1969   *Yanoáma: The Narrative of a White Girl Kidnapped by Amazonian Indians, As Told to Ettore Biocca.* Translated by Dennis Rhodes. New York: Dutton.

Bleier, Ruth
    1984   *Science and Gender: A Critique of Biology and Its Theories on Women.* Elmsford, New York: Pergamon Press.

Boas, Franz
    1928   *Anthropology and Modern Life.* Introduction by Ruth Bunzel. Reprint. New York: Norton, 1962.

Bohannan, Paul
    1963   *Social Anthropology.* New York: Holt, Rinehart & Winston.

Boutilier, James A.
    1984   European Women in the Solomon Islands, 1900–1942: Accommodation and Change on the Pacific Frontier. In *Rethinking Women's Roles: Perspectives from the Pacific,* eds. Denise O'Brien and Sharon W. Tiffany, pp. 173–200. Berkeley and Los Angeles: University of California Press.

Branca, Patricia
    1975   *Silent Sisterhood: Middle Class Women in the Victorian Home.* London: Croom Helm.

Brett, Reverend William H.
    1868   *The Indian Tribes of Guiana: Their Condition and Habits, with Researches into Their Past History, Superstitions, Legends, Antiquities, Languages.* London: Bell and Daldy.
    1881   *Mission Work among the Indian Tribes in the Forests of Guiana.* London: Society for Promoting Christian Knowledge.

Brett, Reverend William H., ed.
    1880   *Legends and Myths of the Aboriginal Indians of British Guiana.* London: William Wells Gardner.

Brown, Judith K.
    1970   Economic Organization and the Position of Women among the Iroquois. In *Women and Society: An Anthropological Reader,* ed. Sharon W. Tiffany, pp. 48–74. Reprint. Montreal: Eden Press, Women's Publications, 1979.

Bullough, Vern L.
    1976   *Sexual Variance in Society and History.* New York: Wiley.

Bullough, Vern, and Martha Voght
    1973   Women, Menstruation, and Nineteenth-Century Medicine. *Bulletin of the History of Medicine* 47(1):66–82.

Butt, Audrey J.
　1957　The Mazaruni Scorpion: A Study of the Symbolic Significance of a Tattoo Pattern among the Akawaio. *Timehri: Journal of the Royal Agricultural and Commercial Society of British Guiana* 36:40–54.

Campbell, I. C.
　1980　Savages Noble and Ignoble: The Preconceptions of Early European Voyagers in Polynesia. *Pacific Studies* 4(1):47–59.

Carew, Jan
　1958　*The Wild Coast.* London: Secker & Warburg.

Carter, Angela
　1978　*The Sadeian Woman and the Ideology of Pornography.* New York: Harper & Row, Harper Colophon Books.

Cavendish, Margaret Lucas [Duchess of Newcastle]
　1666　*The Description of a New World, Called the Blazing World.* London: A Maxwell.

Chagnon, Napoleon A.
　1968a　Yanomamö Social Organization and Warfare. In *War: The Anthropology of Armed Conflict and Aggression,* eds. Morton Fried, Marvin Harris, and Robert Murphy, pp. 109–159. Garden City, New York: Doubleday, for the American Museum of Natural History, Natural History Press.
　1968b　*Yanomamö: The Fierce People.* New York: Holt, Rinehart & Winston.
　1975　Genealogy, Solidarity, and Relatedness: Limits to Local Group Size and Patterns of Fissioning in an Expanding Population. *Yearbook of Physical Anthropology* 19:95–110.
　1977　*Yanomamö: The Fierce People.* 2nd ed. New York: Holt, Rinehart and Winston.
　1983　*Yanomamö: The Fierce People.* 3rd ed. New York: Holt, Rinehart and Winston.

Chagnon, Napoleon A., James V. Neel, Lowell Weitkamp, Henry Gershowitz, and Manuel Ayres
　1970　The Influence of Cultural Factors on the Demography and Pattern of Gene Flow from the Makiritare to the Yanomama Indians. *American Journal of Physical Anthropology* 32:339–350.

Chagnon, Napoleon A., and William Irons, eds.
1979   *Evolutionary Biology and Human Social Behavior: An Anthropological Perspective.* North Scituate, Massachusetts: Duxbury Press.

Chagnon, Napoleon A., and Thomas F. Melancon
1983   Epidemics in a Tribal Population. In *The Impact of Contact: Two Yanomamo Case Studies,* ed. Kenneth M. Kensinger, pp. 53–78. Occasional Paper no. 11. Cambridge, Massachusetts: Cultural Survival.

Chambers, Erve
1981   The Yanomamo and Other Causes: The Ethics of Concern. *Anthropology and Humanism Quarterly* 6 (2/3):25–27.

[Chapman, George?]
1596   De Guiana, Carmen Epicum. In Preface to *A Relation of the Second Voyage to Guiana: Performed and Written in the Year 1596,* by Lawrence Kemys, p. [i]. London: Thomas Dawson.

Clark, Ella E., and Margot Edmonds
1979   *Sacagawea of the Lewis and Clark Expedition.* Berkeley and Los Angeles: University of California Press.

Clark, Lorenne M. G., and Lynda Lange, eds.
1979   *The Sexism of Social and Political Theory: Women and Reproduction from Plato to Nietzsche.* Toronto: University of Toronto Press.

Cohn, Norman
1975   *Europe's Inner Demons: An Enquiry Inspired by the Great Witch-Hunt.* New York: New American Library, Meridian Books.

Colombus, Christopher
1493- *Four Voyages to the New World: Letters and Selected Documents.* Translated and edited by Richard H. Major. Introduction by John E. Fagg. Reprint. New York: Corinth Books, 1961.
1506

Conrad, Joseph
1896   *An Outcast of the Islands.* Reprint. Garden City, New York: Doubleday, Page, 1921.
1899   *Heart of Darkness.* Edited by Robert Kimbrough. 2nd rev. ed. Reprint. New York: Norton, 1971.

Conway, Jill
1972   Stereotypes of Femininity in a Theory of Sexual Evolution. In *Suffer and Be Still: Women in the Victorian Age,* ed.

Martha Vicinus, pp. 140–154. Bloomington: Indiana University Press.

Cott, Nancy F.
 1977 *The Bonds of Womanhood: "Woman's Sphere" in New England, 1780–1835.* New Haven: Yale University Press.
 1978 Passionlessness: An Interpretation of Victorian Sexual Ideology, 1790–1850. *Signs: Journal of Women in Culture and Society* 4(2):219–236.

Coward, Rosalind
 1983 *Patriarchal Precedents: Sexuality and Social Relations.* London: Routledge & Kegan Paul.

Culpepper, Emily E.
 1979 Exploring Menstrual Attitudes. In *Women Look at Biology Looking at Women: A Collection of Feminist Critiques,* eds. Ruth Hubbard, Mary Sue Henifin, Barbara Fried, et al., pp. 135–161. Cambridge, Massachusetts: Schenkman.

Curti, Merle
 1980 *Human Nature in American Thought: A History.* Madison: University of Wisconsin Press.

Curtin, Philip D.
 1964 *The Image of Africa: British Ideas and Action, 1780–1850.* Madison: University of Wisconsin Press.

Dally, Ann
 1982 *Inventing Motherhood: The Consequences of an Ideal.* New York: Schocken Books.

Darwin, Charles
 1859 *On the Origin of Species by Means of Natural Selection; or, the Preservation of Favoured Races in the Struggle for Life.* Reprint. London: John Murray, 1866.

Davis, Shelton H.
 1976 The Yanomamo: Ethnographic Images and Anthropological Responsibilities. In *The Geological Imperative: Anthropology and Development in the Amazon Basin of South America,* by Shelton H. Davis and Robert O. Mathews, pp. 7–23. Cambridge, Massachusetts: Anthropology Resource Center.
 1977 *Victims of the Miracle: Development and the Indians of Brazil.* Cambridge: Cambridge University Press.

Daws, Gavan
 1980 *A Dream of Islands: Voyages of Self-Discovery in the South Seas.* New York: Norton.

de Beauvoir, Simone
   1952   *The Second Sex.* Translated and edited by H. M. Parshley. New York: Random House, Vintage Books.

Degler, Carl N.
   1974   What Ought To Be and What Was: Women's Sexuality in the Nineteenth Century. *American Historical Review* 79:1467–1490.

Delamont, Sara, and Lorna Duffin, eds.
   1978   *The Nineteenth-Century Woman: Her Cultural and Physical World.* London: Croom Helm.

Divale, William Tulio, and Marvin Harris
   1976   Population, Warfare, and the Male Supremacist Complex. *American Anthropologist* 78(3):521–538.

Donne, John
   1633   Satyre IV. In *Complete Poetry and Selected Prose.* Edited by John Hayward. Reprint. London: Nonesuch Press, 1929.

Douglas, Mary
   1980   *Edward Evans-Pritchard.* Harmondsworth, Middlesex, England: Penguin Books.

Doyle, Sir Arthur Conan
   1912   *The Lost World.* New York: Hodder & Stoughton.

Drayton, Michael
   1612–1622   *Poly-Olbion.* Vol. 4. Edited by John William Hebel. Reprint. Oxford: Basic Blackwell, 1933.

Drummond, Lee
   1977   Structure and Process in the Interpretation of South American Myth: The Arawak Dog Spirit People. *American Anthropologist* 79(4):842–868.

Dudley, Edward, and Maximillian E. Novak, eds.
   1972   *The Wild Man Within: An Image in Western Thought from the Renaissance to Romanticism.* Pittsburgh: University of Pittsburgh Press.

Duffin, Lorna
   1978   Prisoners of Progress: Women and Evolution. In *The Nineteenth-Century Woman: Her Cultural and Physical World*, eds. Sara Delamont and Lorna Duffin, pp. 57–91. London: Croom Helm.

Dumont, Jean-Paul
   1978   *The Headman and I: Ambiguity and Ambivalence in the Fieldworking Experience.* Austin: University of Texas Press.

Dworkin, Andrea
- 1976 *Our Blood: Prophecies and Discourses on Sexual Politics.* New York: Harper & Row.
- 1981 *Pornography: Men Possessing Women.* New York: Putnam, Perigree Books.

Ehrenreich, Barbara, and Deirdre English
- 1978 The "Sick" Women of the Upper Classes. In *The Cultural Crisis of Modern Medicine,* ed. John Ehrenreich, pp. 123–143. New York: Monthly Review Press.

Eichler, Margrit
- 1980 *The Double Standard: A Feminist Critique of Feminist Social Science.* New York: St. Martin's Press.

Eisenstein, Zillah
- 1981 *The Radical Future of Liberal Feminism.* New York: Longman.

Elkin, A. P.
- 1939 Introduction to *Aboriginal Woman: Sacred and Profane,* by Phyllis M. Kaberry, pp. xvii–xxxi. London: George Routledge and Sons.

Elshtain, Jean Bethke
- 1981 *Public Man, Private Woman: Women in Social and Political Thought.* Princeton, New Jersey: Princeton University Press.
- 1983 Coming of Age in America: Why the Attack on Margaret Mead? *The Progressive* 47 (October):33–35.

Engels, Frederick
- 1884 *The Origin of the Family, Private Property, and the State.* Edited by Eleanor Burke Leacock. Reprint. New York: International, 1972.

Ernster, Virginia
- 1975 American Menstrual Expressions. *Sex Roles* 1(1):3–13.

Etienne, Mona, and Eleanor Leacock, eds.
- 1980 *Women and Colonization: Anthropological Perspectives.* Brooklyn, New York: Bergin, Praeger Special Studies.

Evans-Pritchard, E. E.
- 1938 *Some Aspects of Marriage and the Family among the Nuer.* Reprint. Rhodes-Livingstone Papers, no. 11. Livingstone, Northern Rhodesia: The Rhodes-Livingstone Institute, 1945.
- 1940a *The Nuer: A Description of the Modes of Livelihood and Polit-*

ical Institutions of a Nilotic People. New York: Oxford University Press.

1940b The Nuer of the Southern Sudan. In *African Political Systems,* eds. M. Fortes and E. E. Evans-Pritchard, pp. 272–296. London: Oxford University Press, for the International African Institute.

1947 A Note on Courtship among the Nuer. *Sudan Notes and Records* 28:115–126.

1950 The Nuer Family. *Sudan Notes and Records* 31:21–42.

1951 *Kinship and Marriage among the Nuer.* Oxford: At the Clarendon Press.

1965 The Position of Women in Primitive Societies and in Our Own. In *The Position of Women in Primitive Societies and Other Essays in Social Anthropology,* by E. E. Evans-Pritchard, pp. 37–58. New York: Macmillian, Free Press.

1973a Some Reminiscences and Reflections on Fieldwork. *Journal of the Anthropological Society of Oxford* 4:1–12.

1973b Genesis of a Social Anthropologist: An Autobiographical Note. *The New Diffusionist* 11(3):17–23.

Faderman, Lillian

1981 *Surpassing the Love of Men: Romantic Friendship and Love between Women from the Renaissance to the Present.* New York: Morrow.

Fairchild, Hoxie Neale

1928 *The Noble Savage: A Study in Romantic Naturalism.* New York: Columbia University Press.

Farabee, William C.

1918 *The Central Arawaks.* Vol. 9. Philadelphia: University Museum.

Fausto-Sterling, Anne

1981 Women and Science. *Women's Studies International Quarterly* 4(1):41–50.

Fee, Elizabeth

1974 The Sexual Politics of Victorian Social Anthropology. In *Clio's Consciousness Raised: New Perspectives on the History of Women,* eds. Mary S. Hartman and Lois W. Banner, pp. 86–102. New York: Harper & Row, Colophon Books.

1976 Science and the Woman Problem: Historical Perspectives. In *Sex Differences: Social and Biological Perspectives,*

ed. Michael S. Teitelbaum, pp. 175–223. Garden City, New York: Doubleday, Anchor Press.
1980 Nineteenth-Century Craniology: The Study of the Female Skull. *Bulletin of the History of Medicine* 53:415–433.
Feil, Daryl Keith
1981 The Bride in Bridewealth: A Case from the New Guinea Highlands. *Ethnology* 20(1):63–75.
Fetterley, Judith
1983 Impersonating "Little Women": The Radicalism of Alcott's *Behind a Mask*. *Women's Studies: An Interdisciplinary Journal* 10 (1):1–14.
Firth, Raymond
1967 Introduction to *A Diary in the Strict Sense of the Term*, by Bronislaw Malinowski, pp. xi–xix. Preface by Valetta Malinowska. Translated by Norbert Guterman. New York: Harcourt, Brace, & World.
Fluehr-Lobban, Carolyn
1979 A Marxist Reappraisal of the Matriarchate. *Current Anthropology* 20(2):341–359.
Foucault, Michel
1972 *The Archaeology of Knowledge.* Translated by A. M. Sheridan Smith. New York: Random House, Pantheon Books.
1978 *The History of Sexuality, Vol. I: An Introduction.* Translated by Robert Hurley. New York: Random House, Pantheon Books.
Freeman, Derek
1983 *Margaret Mead and Samoa: The Making and Unmaking of an Anthropological Myth.* Cambridge: Harvard University Press.
Freeman, James M.
1979 *Untouchable: An Indian Life History.* Stanford: Stanford University Press.
Gardiner, Judith Kegan
1980 Aphra Behn: Sexuality and Self-Respect. *Women's Studies: An Interdisciplinary Journal* 7(1/2):67–78.
Gardner, Susan
1977 For Love and Money: Early Writings of Beatrice Grimshaw, Colonial Papua's Woman of Letters. *New Litera-*

ture Review: Special Issue, Post-Colonial Literature, pp. 10–20. Canberra.

Gay, Peter
1984 *The Bourgeois Experience: Victoria to Freud. Vol. 1, Education of the Senses.* New York: Oxford University Press.

Gerbi, Antonello
1973 *The Dispute of the New World: The History of a Polemic, 1750–1900.* Revised and enlarged ed. Translated by Jeremy Moyle. Pittsburgh: University of Pittsburgh Press.

Gilbert, Sandra M., and Susan Gubar
1979 *The Madwoman in the Attic: The Woman Writer and the Nineteenth-Century Literary Imagination.* New Haven: Yale University Press.

Gillin, John
1936 *The Barama River Caribs of British Guiana.* Papers of the Peabody Museum, Vol. 14, no. 2. Cambridge, Massachusetts: Peabody Museum of American Archaeology and Ethnology.

Gilman, Charlotte Perkins
1915 *Herland.* Introduction by Ann J. Lane. Reprint. New York: Random House, Pantheon Books, 1979.

Glacken, Clarence J.
1967 *Traces on the Rhodian Shore: Nature and Culture in Western Thought from Ancient Times to the End of the Eighteenth Century.* Berkeley and Los Angeles: University of California Press.

Glennon, Lynda M.
1979 *Women and Dualism: A Sociology of Knowledge Analysis.* New York: Longman.

Goldberg, Steven
1974 *The Inevitability of Patriarchy.* New York: Morrow.

Golde, Peggy, ed.
1970 *Women in the Field: Anthropological Experiences.* Chicago: Aldine.

Gonzalez, Nancie L.
1984 The Anthropologist as Female Head of Household. *Feminist Studies* 10(1):97–114.

Goodale, Jane C.
1962 Marriage Contracts among the Tiwi. *Ethnology* 1(4):452–466.

1971 *Tiwi Wives: A Study of the Women of Melville Island, North Australia.* Seattle: University of Washington Press.

Goreau, Angeline
1980 *Reconstructing Aphra: A Social Biography of Aphra Behn.* New York: Dial Press.

Gough, Kathleen
1971 Nuer Kinship: A Re-Examination. In *The Translation of Culture: Essays to E. E. Evans-Pritchard,* ed. T. O. Beidelman, pp. 79–121. London: Tavistock Publications.

Grimshaw, Beatrice
[1927] *Eyes in the Corner and Other Stories.* London: Hurst & Blackett.

Grimshaw, Patricia
1983 "Christian Woman, Pious Wife, Faithful Mother, Devoted Missionary": Conflicts in Roles of American Missionary Women in Nineteenth-Century Hawaii. *Feminist Studies* 9(3):489–521.

Grumet, Robert Steven
1980 Sunksquaws, Shamans, and Tradeswomen: Middle Atlantic Coastal Algonkian Women during the Seventeenth and Eighteenth Centuries. In *Women and Colonization: Anthropological Perspectives,* eds. Mona Etienne and Eleanor Leacock, pp. 43-62. Brooklyn, New York: Bergin, Praeger Special Studies.

Guillaumin, Colette
1981 The Practice of Power and Belief in Nature: Part I, The Appropriation of Women. *Feminist Issues* 1(2):3–28.

Guppy, Nicholas
1958 *Wai-Wai: Through the Forests North of the Amazon.* London: John Murray.

Hall, Joseph
1597 *Satires.* Reprint. London: C. Whittingham, for R. Triphook, 1824.

Hammond, Dorothy, and Alta Jablow
1970 *The Africa That Never Was: Four Centuries of British Writing about Africa.* New York: Twayne.

Handler, Richard
1983 The Dainty and the Hungry Man: Literature and Anthropology in the Work of Edward Sapir. In *Observers Observed: Essays on Ethnographic Fieldwork,* ed. George W.

Stocking, pp. 208–231. Madison: University of Wisconsin Press.

Harding, Sandra, and Merrill B. Hintikka, eds.
   1983   *Discovering Reality: Feminist Perspectives on Epistemology, Metaphysics, Methodology, and Philosophy of Science.* Dordrecht, Holland: D. Reidel.

Harrell, Barbara B.
   1981   Lactation and Menstruation in Cultural Perspective. *American Anthropologist* 83(4):796–823.

Harris, Marvin
   1972   Women's Fib. *Natural History* 81(May):20–22.
   1974   *Cows, Pigs, Wars, and Witches: The Riddles of Culture.* New York: Random House, Vintage Books.
   1977   *Cannibals and Kings: The Origins of Cultures.* New York: Random House.

Harris, Wilson
   1968   *Palace of the Peacock.* London: Faber and Faber.

Hart, C. W. M.
   1954   The Sons of Turimpi. *American Anthropologist* 56(2):242–261, part 1.

Hart, C. W. M., and Arnold R. Pilling
   1960   *The Tiwi of North Australia: Fieldwork Edition.* Reprint. New York: Holt, Rinehart & Winston, 1979.

Hegel, Georg Wilhelm Friedrich
   1837   *Lectures on the Philosophy of World History: Introduction, Reason in History.* Translated from the German edition of Johannes Hoffmeister by H. B. Nisbet. Reprint. Cambridge: Cambridge University Press, 1975.

Henfrey, Colin
   1965   *Through Indian Eyes: A Journey among the Indian Tribes of Guiana.* New York: Holt, Rinehart & Winston.

Henry, Jules
   1963   *Culture against Man.* New York: Random House.

Herzog, Kristin
   1983   *Women, Ethnics, and Exotics: Images of Power in Mid-Nineteenth-Century American Fiction.* Knoxville: University of Tennessee Press.

Hill, Mary A.
   1980   *Charlotte Perkins Gilman: The Making of a Radical Feminist, 1860–1896.* Philadelphia: Temple University Press.

Holcombe, Lee
  1973 *Victorian Ladies at Work: Middle-Class Working Women in England and Wales, 1850–1914.* Hamden, Connecticut: Shoe String Press, Archon Books.
Honour, Hugh
  1975 *The New Golden Land: European Images of America from the Discoveries to the Present Time.* New York: Random House, Pantheon Books.
Houghton, Walter E.
  1957 *The Victorian Frame of Mind, 1830–1970.* New Haven: Yale University Press, for Wellesley College.
Hrdy, Sarah Blaffer
  1981 *The Woman That Never Evolved.* Cambridge: Harvard University Press.
Hubbard, Ruth, Mary Sue Henifin, and Barbara Fried, eds.
  1982 *Biological Woman—The Convenient Myth: A Collection of Feminist Essays and a Comprehensive Bibliography.* Cambridge, Massachusetts: Schenkman.
Hudson, William Henry
  1904 *Green Mansions: A Romance of the Tropical Forest.* Reprint. New York: Random House, Modern Library, 1944.
Im Thurn, Sir Everard Ferdinand
  1883 *Among the Indians of Guiana: Being Sketches Chiefly Anthropologic from the Interior of British Guiana.* London: Kegan Paul, Trench.
Inglis, Amirah
  1974 *The White Women's Protection Ordinance: Sexual Anxiety and Politics in Papua.* London: Chatto and Windus, for Sussex University Press.
Jaggar, Alison M.
  1983 *Feminist Politics and Human Nature.* Totowa, New Jersey: Rowman & Allanheld.
Johnson, Douglas
  1979 Colonial Policy and Prophets: The "Nuer Settlement," 1929–1930. *Journal of the Anthropological Society of Oxford* 10(1):1–20.
Kaberry, Phyllis M.
  1939 *Aboriginal Woman: Sacred and Profane.* London: George Routledge and Sons.
  1952 *Women of the Grassfields: A Study of the Economic Position of*

Women in Bamenda, British Cameroons. London: Her Majesty's Stationery Office.

Kandell, Jonathan
1984   Passage through El Dorado: Traveling the World's Last Great Wilderness. New York: Morrow.

Keen, Benjamin
1971   The Aztec Image in Western Thought. New Brunswick, New Jersey: Rutgers University Press.

Kemys, Lawrence
1596   A Relation of the Second Voyage to Guiana: Performed and Written in the Year 1596. London: Thomas Dawson.

Kern, Louis J.
1981   An Ordered Love: Sex Roles and Sexuality in Victorian Utopias—The Shakers, the Mormons, and the Oneida Community. Chapel Hill: University of North Carolina Press.

Kiernan, E. Victor Gordon
1969   The Lords of Human Kind: Black Man, Yellow Man, and White Man in an Age of Empire. Boston: Little, Brown.

Kleinbaum, Abby Wettan
1983   The War against the Amazons. New York: New Press, McGraw-Hill.

Kolodny, Annette
1975   The Lay of the Land: Metaphor as Experience and History in American Life and Letters. Chapel Hill: University of North Carolina Press.
1984   The Land Before Her: Fantasy and Experience of the American Frontiers, 1630–1860. Chapel Hill: University of North Carolina Press.

Krige, Eileen Jensen
1974   Woman-Marriage, with Special Reference to the Lovedu—Its Significance for the Definition of Marriage. In Women and Society: An Anthropological Reader, ed. Sharon W. Tiffany, pp. 208–237. Reprint. Montreal: Eden Press, Women's Publications, 1979.

Kuper, Adam
1973   Anthropologists and Anthropology: The British School, 1922–1972. New York: Pica Press.

LaBelle, Beverly
1980   The Propaganda of Misogyny. In Take Back the Night: Women on Pornography, ed. Laura Lederer, pp. 174–178. New York: Morrow.

Lane, Ann J.
1977   Mary Ritter Beard: An Appraisal of Her Life and Work. In *Mary Ritter Beard: A Sourcebook*, ed. Ann J. Lane, pp. 1–72. New York: Schocken Books.
1980   The Fictional World of Charlotte Perkins Gilman. In *The Charlotte Perkins Gilman Reader: "The Yellow Wallpaper" and Other Fiction*, ed. Ann J. Lane, pp. ix–xli. New York: Random House, Pantheon Books.

Laracy, Eugénie, and Hugh Laracy
1977   Beatrice Grimshaw: Pride and Prejudice in Papua. *Journal of Pacific History* 12(3/4):154–175.

La Varre, William J.
1935   *Gold, Diamonds, and Orchids*. New York: Fleming H. Revell.

Lawrence, D. H.
1917   New Heaven and Earth. In *Look! We Have Come Through!* by D. H. Lawrence, pp. 125–136. London: Chatto & Windus.

Leach, Edmund
1964   Anthropological Aspects of Language: Animal Categories and Verbal Abuse. In *Mythology: Selected Readings*, ed. Pierre Maranda, pp. 39–67. Reprint. Harmondsworth, Middlesex, England: Penguin Books, 1972.

Leacock, Eleanor Burke
1972   Introduction to *The Origin of the Family, Private Property, and the State*, by Frederick Engels, pp. 7–67. Edited by Eleanor Burke Leacock. New York: International.
1981   *Myths of Male Dominance: Collected Articles on Women Cross-Culturally*. New York: Monthly Review Press.
1983a   Interpreting the Origins of Gender Inequality: Conceptual and Historical Problems. *Dialectical Anthropology* 7:263–284.
1983b   Ideologies of Male Dominance as Divide and Rule Politics: An Anthropologist's View. In *Woman's Nature: Rationalizations of Inequality*, eds. Marian Lowe and Ruth Hubbard, pp. 111–121. Elmsford, New York: Pergamon Press.

Leibowitz, Lila
1983   Origins of the Sexual Division of Labor. In *Woman's Nature: Rationalizations of Inequality*, eds. Marian Lowe and

Ruth Hubbard, pp. 123–147. Elmsford, New York: Pergamon Press.

Levin, Harry
   1969   *The Myth of the Golden Age in the Renaissance.* Bloomington: Indiana University Press.

Lévi-Strauss, Claude
   1961   *Tristes Tropiques: An Anthropological Study of Primitive Societies in Brazil.* Translated by John Russell. New York: Atheneum.
   1969   *The Elementary Structures of Kinship.* Rev. ed. Edited by Rodney Needham. Translated by James Harle Bell, John Richard Von Sturmer, and Rodney Needham. Boston: Beacon Press.

Lewis, I. M.
   1976   *Social Anthropology in Perspective: The Relevance of Social Anthropology.* Harmondsworth, Middlesex, England: Penguin Books.

Lizot, Jacques
   1976a   *Le Cercle des Feux: Faits et Dits des Indiens Yanomami.* Paris: Éditions du Seuil.
   1976b   *The Yanomami in the Face of Ethnocide.* Translated and edited by Roger Moody. IWGA Document no. 22. Copenhagen: International Work Group for Indigenous Affairs.
   1977   Population, Resources, and Warfare among the Yanomami. *Man* (new series) 12(3/4):497–517.

Llosa, Mario Vargas
   1968   *The Green House.* Translated by Gregory Rabassa. New York: Avon Books, Bard Books.

Locke, John
   1690   *The Second Treatise of Civil Government and a Letter Concerning Toleration.* Edited and introduction by John W. Gough. Reprint. Oxford: Basil Blackwell, 1946.

Lowe, Donald M.
   1982   *History of Bourgeois Perception.* Chicago: University of Chicago Press.

Lowe, Marian, and Ruth Hubbard, eds.
   1983   *Woman's Nature: Rationalizations of Inequality.* Elmsford, New York: Pergamon Press.

Lurie, Nancy Oestreich, ed.
   1961   *Mountain Wolf Woman, Sister of Crashing Thunder: The*

Autobiography of a Winnebago Indian. Ann Arbor: University of Michigan Press.

McCann, Franklin T.
1951 *English Discovery of America to 1585.* New York: King's Crown Press.

MacCormack, Carol P., and Marilyn Strathern, eds.
1980 *Nature, Culture, and Gender.* Cambridge: Cambridge University Press.

McMillan, Carol
1982 *Women, Reason, and Nature: Some Philosophical Problems with Feminism.* Princeton, New Jersey: Princeton University Press.

Malinowski, Bronislaw
1929 *The Sexual Life of Savages in North-Western Melanesia: An Ethnographic Account of Courtship, Marriage, and Family Life among the Natives of the Trobriand Islands, British New Guinea.* New York: Harcourt, Brace & World, Harvest Books.
1967 *A Diary in the Strict Sense of the Term.* Preface by Valetta Malinowska. Introduction by Raymond Firth. Translated by Norbert Guterman. New York: Harcourt, Brace & World.

Mannoni, O.
1964 *Prospero and Caliban: The Psychology of Colonization.* 2nd ed. New York: Frederick A. Praeger.

Marcuse, Herbert
1955 *Eros and Civilization: A Philosophical Inquiry into Freud.* Boston: Beacon Press.

Martin M. Kay, and Barbara Voorhies
1975 *Female of the Species.* New York: Columbia University Press.

Martin, Wendy
1971 Seduced and Abandoned in the New World: The Image of Woman in American Fiction. In *Woman in Sexist Society: Studies in Power and Powerlessness*, eds. Vivian Gornick and Barbara K. Moran, pp. 226–239. New York: Basic Books.

Mathieu, Nicole-Claude
1978 Man-Culture and Woman-Nature? Translated by D. M. Leonard Barker. *Women's Studies International Quarterly* 1(1):55–65.

1980 Masculinity/Femininity. *Feminist Issues* 1(1):51–69.

Mead, Margaret
 1928 *Coming of Age in Samoa: A Psychological Study of Primitive Youth for Western Civilization.* Reprint. New York: Morrow, Morrow Quill Paperbacks, 1961.
 1935 *Sex and Temperament in Three Primitive Societies.* New York: Morrow.
 1949 *Male and Female: A Study of the Sexes in a Changing World.* New York: Morrow.
 1972 *Blackberry Winter: My Earlier Years.* New York: Simon and Schuster, Touchstone Books.
 1977 *Letters from the Field, 1925–1975.* New York: Harper & Row, Harper Colophon Books.

Medicine, Beatrice
 1983 Indian Women: Tribal Identity as Status Quo. In *Woman's Nature: Rationalizations of Inequality*, eds. Marion Lowe and Ruth Hubbard, pp. 63–73. Elmsford, New York: Pergamon Press.

Meggers, Betty J.
 1971 *Amazonia: Man and Culture in a Counterfeit Paradise.* Chicago: Aldine-Atherton.

Meggitt, M. J.
 1962 *Desert People: A Study of the Walbiri Aborigines of Central Australia.* Chicago: University of Chicago Press.
 1964 Male-Female Relationships in the Highlands of Australian New Guinea. *American Anthropologist* 66(4):204–224, part 2.

Meigs, Anna S.
 1976 Male Pregnancy and the Reduction of Sexual Opposition in a New Guinea Highlands Society. *Ethnology* 15(4):393–407.

Melville, Herman
 1846 *Typee: A Peep at Polynesian Life.* Edited by Harrison Hayford, Hershel Parker, and G. Thomas Tanselle. Northwestern-Newberry ed. Reprint. Evanston and Chicago: Northwestern University Press and the Newberry Library, 1968.
 1847 *Omoo: A Narrative of Adventures in the South Seas.* Edited by Harrison Hayford, Hershel Parker, and G. Thomas Tanselle. Northwestern-Newberry ed. Reprint. Evan-

ston and Chicago: Northwestern University Press and the Newberry Library, 1968.

Merchant, Carolyn
1980 *The Death of Nature: Women, Ecology, and the Scientific Revolution.* New York: Harper & Row.

Milton, John
1667 *Milton's Paradise Lost.* Edited by James Prendeville. Reprint. London: Samuel Holdsworth, 1840.

Mittelholzer, Edgar
1941 *Corentyne Thunder.* Reprint. London: Heinemann Educational Books, 1970.

Modell, Judith Schachter
1983 *Ruth Benedict: Patterns of a Life.* Philadelphia: University of Pennsylvania Press.

Modleski, Tania
1982 *Loving with a Vengeance: Mass-Produced Fantasies for Women.* Hamden, Connecticut: Shoe String Press, Archon Books.

Montaigne, Michel Eyquem de
1580 *The Autobiography of Michel de Montaigne.* Translated by Marvin Lowenthal. Reprint. New York: Vintage Books, 1935.

More, Sir Thomas
1516 *Sir Thomas More's Utopia.* Edited and introduction by J. Churton Collins. Reprint. Oxford: Clarendon Press, 1904.

Morgan, Lewis Henry
1877 *Ancient Society; or, Researches in the Lines of Human Progress from Savagery through Barbarism to Civilization.* Edited by Eleanor Burke Leacock. Reprint. Cleveland: World, Meridian Books, 1963.

Morris, Desmond
1967 *The Naked Ape.* New York: Dell.

Mosedale, Susan Sleeth
1978 Science Corrupted: Victorian Biologists Consider "The Woman Question." *Journal of the History of Biology* 11(1):1–55.

Murphy, Robert F.
1959 Social Structure and Sex Antagonism. In *Peoples and Cultures of Native South America: An Anthropological Reader,*

ed. Daniel R. Gross, pp. 213–224. Reprint. Garden City, New York: Doubleday, The Natural History Press, for the American Museum of Natural History, 1973.
1960   *Headhunter's Heritage: Social and Economic Change among the Mundurucú Indians.* Berkeley and Los Angeles: University of California Press.

Murphy, Yolanda, and Robert F. Murphy
1974   *Women of the Forest.* New York: Columbia University Press.

Murray, Janet Horowitz
1982   *Strong-Minded Women: And Other Lost Voices from Nineteenth-Century England.* New York: Random House, Pantheon Books.

Nachman, Steven R.
1983   Lies My Informants Told Me. Paper presented at 82nd annual meeting of the American Anthropological Association, Chicago.

Naipaul, Shiva
1981   *Journey to Nowhere: A New World Tragedy.* New York: Simon & Schuster.
1983   *Love and Death in a Hot Country.* New York: Viking Press.

Naipaul, V. S.
1962   *The Middle Passage: Impressions of Five Societies—British, French, and Dutch—in the West Indies and South America.* New York: Random House, Vintage Books.
1967   Columbus and Crusoe. In *The Overcrowded Barracoon,* by V. S. Naipaul, pp. 203–207. Reprint. New York: Knopf, 1972.
1969   *The Loss of El Dorado: A History.* Harmondsworth, Middlesex, England: Penguin Books.

Nardi, Bonnie A.
1984   The Height of Her Powers: Margaret Mead's Samoa. *Feminist Studies* 10(2):323–337.

Nash, June
1978   The Aztecs and the Ideology of Male Dominance. *Signs: Journal of Women in Culture and Society* 4(2):349–362.

Needham, Rodney
1974   Surmise, Discovery, and Rhetoric. In *Remarks and Inventions: Skeptical Essays about Kinship* by Rodney Needham, pp. 109–162. London: Tavistock Publications.

Nichols, William
1979- Lewis and Clark Probe the Heart of Darkness. *American*
1980 *Scholar* 49 (winter):94–101.
Norwood, Victor G. C.
1960 *A Hand Full of Diamonds: Further Adventures and Experiences in the Jungles and Diamond Fields of Guiana and Brazil.* 1st ed. London: T. V. Boardman.
Oboler, Regina Smith
1980 Is the Female Husband a Man? Woman/Woman Marriage among the Nandi of Kenya. *Ethnology* 19(1):69–88.
O'Brien, Denise
1977 Female Husbands in Southern Bantu Societies. In *Sexual Stratification: A Cross-Cultural View*, ed. Alice Schlegel, pp. 109–126. New York: Columbia University Press.
1984 "Women Never Hunt": The Portrayal of Women in Melanesian Ethnography. In *Rethinking Women's Roles: Perspectives from the Pacific*, eds. Denise O'Brien and Sharon W. Tiffany, pp. 53–70. Berkeley and Los Angeles: University of California Press.
n.d. Images of Women in the South Seas. Unpublished manuscript.
O'Brien, Mary
1981 *The Politics of Reproduction.* Boston: Routledge & Kegan Paul.
Ogbu, John U.
1978 African Bridewealth and Women's Status. *American Ethnologist* 5(2):241–262.
Okin, Susan Moller
1979 *Women in Western Political Thought.* Princeton, New Jersey: Princeton University Press.
Ortner, Sherry B.
1974 Is Female to Male as Nature Is to Culture? In *Woman, Culture, and Society*, eds. Michelle Zimbalist Rosaldo and Louise Lamphere, pp. 67–87. Stanford: Stanford University Press.
Ortner, Sherry B., and Harriet Whitehead, eds.
1981 *Sexual Meanings: The Cultural Construction of Gender and Sexuality.* Cambridge: Cambridge University Press.
Paloma, Dolores
1980 Margaret Cavendish: Defining the Female Self. *Women's Studies: An Interdisciplinary Journal* 7 (1/2):55–66.

Parsons, Elsie Clews
  1913   *The Old-Fashioned Woman: Primitive Fancies about the Sex.* New York: Putnam.
Payne, Edward John
  1900   Introduction. In *Voyages of the Elizabethan Seamen to America: Select Narratives from the "Principal Navigations" of Hakluyt.* Edited by Edward John Payne, pp. vii–xlix. 2nd ed., 2nd series. Oxford: Clarendon Press.
Pearsall, Ronald
  1977   *Conan Doyle, A Biographical Solution.* New York: St. Martin's Press.
Pichanick, Valerie Kossew
  1980   *Harriet Martineau: The Woman and Her Work, 1802–1876.* Ann Arbor: University of Michigan Press.
Pierce, Christine
  1971   Natural Law Language and Women. In *Woman in Sexist Society: Studies in Power and Powerlessness,* eds. Vivian Gornick and Barbara K. Moran, pp. 160–172. New York: Basic Books.
Poewe, Karla O.
  1981   *Matrilineal Ideology: Male-Female Dynamics in Luapula, Zambia.* London: Academic Press, for the International African Institute.
Poewe, Karla O. [Manda Cesara, pseud.]
  1982   *Reflections of a Woman Anthropologist: No Hiding Place.* London: Academic Press.
Quinn, Naomi
  1977   Anthropological Studies on Women's Status. In *Annual Review of Anthropology.* Vol. 6. Edited by Bernard J. Siegel, pp. 181–225. Stanford: Stanford University Press.
Radcliffe-Brown, A. R.
  1935   Patrilineal and Matrilineal Succession. In *Structure and Function in Primitive Society: Essays and Addresses,* by A. R. Radcliffe-Brown, pp. 32–48. Reprint. New York: Macmillan, Free Press, 1952.
Raleigh, Walter
  1596   *The Discovery of the Large, Rich, and Beautiful Empire of Guiana, with a Relation of the Great and Golden City of Manoa . . . Performed in the Year 1595.* Edited by Sir

Robert H. Schomburgk. Reprint. London: For the Hakluyt Society, 1848.

Ramos, Alcida R.
1979   On Women's Status in Yanoama Societies. *Current Anthropology* 20(1):185–187.

Rattray, R. S.
1923   *Ashanti.* Oxford: At the Clarendon Press.

Redfield, Robert
1953   *The Primitive World and Its Transformations.* Ithaca, New York: Cornell University Press.

Reiter, Rayna R., ed.
1975   *Toward an Anthropology of Women.* New York: Monthly Review Press.

Ribeiro, Darcy
1984   *Maíra.* Translated by E. H. Goodland and Thomas Colchie. New York: Random House, Vintage Books.

Rich, Adrienne
1976   *Of Woman Born: Motherhood as Experience and Institution.* New York: Bantam Books.
1977   Foreword. Conditions for Work: The Common World of Women. In *Working It Out: Twenty-Three Women Writers, Artists, Scientists, and Scholars Talk about Their Lives and Work,* eds. Sara Ruddick and Pamela Daniels, pp. xiii–xxiv. New York: Random House, Pantheon Books.

Richards, Audrey
1968   In Darkest Malinowski. *The Cambridge Review* (19 January):186–189.

Rodway, James
1894   *In the Guiana Forest: Studies of Nature in Relation to the Struggle for Life.* New York: Scribner.
1899   *In Guiana Wilds: A Study of Two Women.* Boston: L. C. Page.

Rogers, Susan Carol
1978   Woman's Place: A Critical Review of Anthropological Theory. *Comparative Studies in Society and History* 20:123–162.

Rohrlich, Ruby
1980   State Formation in Sumer and the Subjugation of Women. *Feminist Studies* 6(1):76–102.

Rohrlich-Leavitt, Ruby
   1976   Peaceable Primates and Gentle People: An Anthropological Approach to Women's Studies. In *Women's Studies: The Social Realities*, ed. Barbara Bellow Watson, pp. 165–202. New York: Harper & Row, Harper's College Press.

Rosaldo, Michelle Zimbalist
   1974   Woman, Culture, and Society: A Theoretical Overview. In *Woman, Culture, and Society*, eds. Michelle Zimbalist Rosaldo and Louise Lamphere, pp. 17–42. Stanford: Stanford University Press.
   1980   The Use and Abuse of Anthropology: Reflections on Feminism and Cross-Cultural Understanding. *Signs: Journal of Women in Culture and Society* 5(3):389–417.
   1983   Moral/Analytic Dilemmas Posed by the Intersection of Feminism and Social Science. In *Social Science as Moral Inquiry*, eds. Norma Haan, Robert N. Bellah, Paul Rabinow, and William M. Sullivan, pp. 76–95. New York: Columbia University Press.

Rosenberg, Charles E.
   1973   Sexuality, Class, and Role in Nineteenth-Century America. *American Quarterly* 25(2):131–153.

Roth, Walter E.
   1915   An Inquiry into the Animism and Folk-Lore of the Guiana Indians. In *U.S. Bureau of American Ethnology, 30th Annual Report, 1908–1909*, pp. 103–386. Washington, D.C.: U.S. Government Printing Office.

Rousseau, Jean Jacques
   1762   *Émile; or, Education*. Translated by Barbara Foxley. Reprint. London: J. M. Dent & Sons, 1911.

Ruby, Jay, ed.
   1982   *A Crack in the Mirror: Reflexive Perspectives in Anthropology*. Philadelphia: University of Pennsylvania Press.

Ruddick, Sara
   1980   Maternal Thinking. *Feminist Studies* 6(2):342–367.

Sacks, Karen
   1974   Engels Revisited: Women, the Organization of Production, and Private Property. In *Woman, Culture, and Society*, eds. Michelle Zimbalist Rosaldo and Louise Lam-

phere, pp. 207–222. Stanford: Stanford University Press.
1979 *Sisters and Wives: The Past and Future of Sexual Equality.* Contributions in Women's Studies, no. 10. Westport, Connecticut: Greenwood Press.

Saffirio, John, and Raymond Hames
1983 The Forest and the Highway. In *The Impact of Contact: Two Yanomamo Case Studies,* ed. Kenneth M. Kensinger, pp. 1–52. Occasional Paper no. 11. Cambridge, Massachusetts: Cultural Survival.

Salter, Elizabeth
1971 *Daisy Bates: "The Great White Queen of the Never Never."* London: Angus and Robertson.

Sanday, Peggy Reeves
1981 *Female Power and Male Dominance: On the Origins of Sexual Inequality.* Cambridge: Cambridge University Press.

Saxton, Martha
1977 *Louisa May: A Modern Biography.* New York: Avon Books.

Sayers, Janet
1982 *Biological Politics: Feminist and Anti-Feminist Perspectives.* London: Tavistock Publications.

Scheper-Hughes, Nancy
1983 Introduction: The Problem of Bias in Androcentric and Feminist Anthropology. *Women's Studies: An Interdisciplinary Journal* 10 (2):109–116.

Schlegel, Alice
1977 Toward a Theory of Sexual Stratification. In *Sexual Stratification: A Cross-Cultural View,* ed. Alice Schlegel, pp. 1–40. New York: Columbia University Press.

Scholte, Bob
1972 Toward a Reflexive and Critical Anthropology. In *Reinventing Anthropology,* ed. Dell Hymes, pp. 430–457. New York: Random House, Vintage Books.

Schomburgk, Moritz Richard
1847– *Travels in British Guiana, 1840–1844.* 2 vols. Translated
1848 and edited by Walter E. Roth. Reprint. Georgetown, British Guiana: *Daily Chronicle* Office, 1922–1923.

Schomburgk, Robert H.
1848 Introduction to *The Discovery of The Large, Rich, and Beau-*

tiful Empire of Guiana, by Walter Raleigh, pp. xiii–lxxv. Edited by Sir Robert H. Schomburgk. Reprint of 1596 ed. London: For the Hakluyt Society.

Schulz, Muriel R.
  1975   The Semantic Derogation of Women. In *Language and Sex: Difference and Dominance*, eds. Barrie Thorne and Nancy Henley, pp. 64–75. Rowley, Massachusetts: Newbury House.

Service, Elman R.
  1971   *Primitive Social Organization: An Evolutionary Perspective.* 2nd ed. New York: Random House.

Shapiro, Judith R.
  1972   *Sex Roles and Social Structure among the Yanomama Indians of Northern Brazil.* Ph.D. dissertation, Columbia University.
  1976   Sexual Hierarchy among the Yanomama. In *Sex and Class in Latin America*, eds. June Nash and Helen Icken Safa, pp. 86–101. New York: Praeger.

Sherman, Julia A., and Evelyn Torton Beck, eds.
  1979   *The Prism of Sex: Essays in the Sociology of Knowledge.* Madison: University of Wisconsin Press.

Shimony, Annemarie
  1980   Women of Influence and Prestige among the Native American Iroquois. In *Unspoken Worlds: Women's Religious Lives in Non-Western Cultures*, eds. Nancy Auer Falk and Rita M. Gross, pp. 243–259. New York: Harper & Row.

Shostak, Marjorie
  1981   *Nisa: The Life and Words of a !Kung Woman.* Cambridge: Harvard University Press.

Singer, Alice
  1973   Marriage Payments and the Exchange of People. *Man* (new series) 8(1):80–92.

Siskind, Janet
  1973a Tropical Forest Hunters and the Economy of Sex. In *Peoples and Cultures of Native South America: An Anthropological Reader*, ed. Daniel R. Gross, pp. 226–240. Garden City, New York: Doubleday, The Natural History Press, for the American Museum of Natural History.

1973b   *To Hunt in the Morning*. New York: Oxford University Press.

Smith, Bonnie G.
1981   *Ladies of the Leisure Class: The Bourgeoises of Northern France in the Nineteenth Century*. Princeton, New Jersey: Princeton University Press.

Smith, F. Barry
1977   Sexuality in Britain, 1800–1900: Some Suggested Revisions. In *A Widening Sphere: Changing Roles of Victorian Women*, ed. Martha Vicinus, pp. 182–198. Bloomington: Indiana University Press.

Smith, Mary F.
1955   *Baba of Karo: A Woman of the Muslim Hausa*. New York: Philosophical Library.

Smith, Raymond T.
1956   *The Negro Family in British Guiana: Family Structure and Social Status in the Villages*. London: Routledge and Paul, in Association with the Institute of Social and Economic Research, University College of the West Indies, Jamaica.

Smith-Rosenberg, Carroll
1975   The Female World of Love and Ritual: Relations between Women in Nineteenth-Century America. *Signs: Journal of Women in Culture and Society* 1(1):1–29.

Smith-Rosenberg, Carroll, and Charles Rosenberg
1973   The Female Animal: Medical and Biological Views of Woman and Her Role in Nineteenth-Century America. *Journal of American History* 60 (2):332–356.

Souza, Márcio
1977   *The Emperor of the Amazon*. Translated by Thomas Colchie. New York: Avon Books, Bard Books.

Spender, Dale
1980   *Man Made Language*. London: Routledge and Kegan Paul.

Stark-Adamec, Cannie, ed.
1981   Special Issue: Women and Science. *International Journal of Women's Studies* 4(4):311–455.

Stearns, Peter N.
1972   Working-Class Women in Britain, 1890–1914. In *Suffer and Be Still: Women in the Victorian Age*, ed. Martha

Vicinus, pp. 100–120. Bloomington: Indiana University Press.

Stern, Madeleine
1975 Introduction. In *Behind a Mask: The Unknown Thrillers of Louisa May Alcott*, ed. Madeleine Stern, pp. vii–xxxiii. New York: Morrow.
1976 Introduction. In *Plots and Counterplots: More Unknown Thrillers of Louisa May Alcott*, ed. Madeleine Stern, pp. 7–29. New York: CBS, Popular Library.

Stevenson, Robert Louis
1900 *In the South Seas: Being an Account of Experiences and Observations in the Marquesas, Paumotus, and Gilbert Islands. . . .* Reprint. Honolulu: University of Hawaii Press, 1971.
1904 *Island Nights' Entertainments.* Reprint. Honolulu: The University Press of Hawaii, 1975.

Stocking, George W., Jr.
1983 The Ethnographer's Magic: Fieldwork in British Anthropology from Tylor to Malinowski. In *Observers Observed: Essays on Ethnographic Fieldwork*, ed. George W. Stocking, Jr., pp. 70–120. Madison: University of Wisconsin Press.

Strathern, Andrew, trans.
1979 *Ongka: A Self-Account by a New Guinea Big-Man.* New York: St. Martin's Press.

Strathern, Marilyn
1980 No Nature, No Culture: The Hagen Case. In *Nature, Culture, and Gender*, eds. Carol P. MacCormack and Marilyn Strathern, pp. 174–222. Cambridge: Cambridge University Press.
1981 Self-Interest and the Social Good: Some Implications of Hagen Gender Imagery. In *Sexual Meanings: The Cultual Construction of Gender and Sexuality*, eds. Sherry B. Ortner and Harriet Whitehead, pp. 166–191. Cambridge: Cambridge University Press.
1984 Domesticity and the Denigration of Women. In *Rethinking Women's Roles: Perspectives from the Pacific*, eds. Denise O'Brien and Sharon W. Tiffany, pp. 13–31. Berkeley and Los Angeles: University of California Press.

Street, Brian V.
  1975   *The Savage in Literature: Representations of "Primitive" Society in English Fiction, 1858–1920.* London: Routledge and Kegan Paul.
Tanner, Nancy Makepeace
  1981   *On Becoming Human.* Cambridge: Cambridge University Press.
Taylor, J. M.
  1979   *Eva Perón: The Myths of a Woman.* Chicago: University of Chicago Press.
Thoreau, Henry David
  1905   *Sir Walter Raleigh.* Edited by Henry Aiken Metcalf. Boston: Bibliophile Society.
Tiffany, Sharon W.
  1978   Models and the Social Anthropology of Women: A Preliminary Assessment. *Man* (new series) 13(1):34–51.
  1979a Introduction: Theoretical Issues in the Anthropological Study of Women. In *Women and Society: An Anthropological Reader,* ed. Sharon W. Tiffany, pp. 1–35. Montreal: Eden Press, Women's Publications.
  1979b Women, Power, and the Anthropology of Politics: A Review. *International Journal of Women's Studies* 2(5):430–442.
  1982a The Power of Matriarchal Ideas. *International Journal of Women's Studies* 5(2):138–147.
  1982b *Women, Work, and Motherhood: The Power of Female Sexuality in the Workplace.* Englewood Cliffs, New Jersey: Prentice-Hall, Spectrum Books.
  1982c Women in Cross-Cultural Perspective: A Guide to Recent Anthropological Literature. *Women's Studies International Forum* 5(5):497–502.
  1984   Introduction: Feminist Perceptions in Anthropology. In *Rethinking Women's Roles: Perspectives from the Pacific,* eds. Denise O'Brien and Sharon W. Tiffany, pp. 1–11. Berkeley and Los Angeles: University of California Press.
  n.d.a Feminist Frameworks and Cross-Cultural Understanding: Reflections on Anthropological Discourse about Women. Unpublished manuscript.
  n.d.b Paradise and Perdition in the South Seas: An Inquiry

into the Anthropological Romance of Samoa. Unpublished manuscript.

n.d.c   Paradigms of Power: Feminist Reflections on the Anthropology of Women in Pacific Island Societies. Unpublished manuscript.

n.d.d   *Women and Their Bodies: The Politics of Sex and Motherhood in Cultural Perspective.* Unpublished manuscript.

Tiger, Lionel
    1969   *Men in Groups.* New York: Random House, Vintage Books.

Tiger, Lionel, and Robin Fox
    1971   *The Imperial Animal.* New York: Dell, Delta Books.

Trachtenberg, Alan
    1976   Review of *The New Golden Land: European Images of America from the Discoveries to the Present Time,* by Hugh Honour. *The New York Times Book Review* 75(43):27–29.

Ulrich, Laurel Thatcher
    1982   *Good Wives: Image and Reality in the Lives of Women in Northern New England, 1650–1750.* New York: Oxford University Press.

Van Allen, Judith
    1972   "Sitting on a Man": Colonialism and the Lost Political Institutions of Igbo Women. In *Women and Society: An Anthropological Reader,* ed. Sharon W. Tiffany, pp. 163–187. Reprint. Montreal: Eden Press, Women's Publications, 1979.

Vespucci, Amerigo
    1503   *Mundus Novus: Letter to Lorenzo Pietro di Medici.* Translated by George Tyler Northup. Reprint. Princeton, New Jersey: Princeton University Press, 1916a.
    1504.   *Letter to Piero Soderini.* Introduction and translation by George Tyler Northup. Reprint. Princeton, New Jersey: Princeton University Press, 1916b.

Vicinus, Martha
    1972a   Introduction: The Perfect Victorian Lady. In *Suffer and Be Still: Women in the Victorian Age.* ed. Martha Vicinus, pp. vii–xv. Bloomington: Indiana University Press.

Vicinus, Martha, ed.
    1972b   *Suffer and Be Still: Women in the Victorian Age.* Bloomington: Indiana University Press.

1977 *A Widening Sphere: Changing Roles of Victorian Women.* Bloomington: Indiana University Press.

Voltaire, François Marie Arouet de
1759 Candide, or Optimism. In *Candide, Zadig, and Selected Stories.* Introduction and translation by Donald M. Frame. Reprint. New York: New American Library, Signet Books, 1961.

Walkowitz, Judith R.
1980 *Prostitution and Victorian Society: Women, Class, and the State.* Cambridge: Cambridge University Press.

Warner, Marina
1981 *Joan of Arc: The Image of Female Heroism.* New York: Random House, Vintage Books.

Waterton, Charles
1825 *Wanderings in South America, The North-West of the United States, and the Antilles in the Years 1812, 1816, 1820, and 1824.* Reprint. New York: Sturgis & Walton, 1909.

Watt, Ian
1979 *Conrad in the Nineteenth Century.* Berkeley and Los Angeles: University of California Press.

Waugh, Evelyn
1934a *Ninety-Two Days.* London: Duckworth.
1934b *A Handful of Dust.* New York: Farrar & Rinehart.
1976 *The Diaries of Evelyn Waugh.* Edited by Michael Davie. Boston: Little, Brown.

Wax, Murray L.
1972 Tenting with Malinowski. *American Sociological Review* 37 (1):1–13.

Webber, Lieutenant Colonel George Daniel
1873 *British Guiana: The Essequibo and Potaro Rivers, with an Account of a Visit to the Recently-Discovered Kaieteur Falls.* London: Edward Stanford.

Webster, Paula
1975 Matriarchy: A Vision of Power. In *Toward an Anthropology of Women,* ed. Rayna R. Reiter, pp. 141–156. New York: Monthly Review Press.

Weeks, Jeffery
1981 *Sex, Politics, and Society: The Regulation of Sexuality since 1800.* London: Longman Group.

Weiner, Annette B.

1976   *Women of Value, Men of Renown: New Perspectives in Trobriand Exchange.* Austin: University of Texas Press.

Welter, Barbara
- 1966a   Anti-Intellectualism and the American Woman, 1800–1860. *Mid-America* 48:258–270.
- 1966b   The Cult of True Womanhood, 1820–1860. *American Quarterly* 18(2):151–174, part 1.

Whitbeck, Caroline
- 1976   Theories of Sex Difference. In *Women and Philosophy: Toward a Theory of Liberation,* eds. Carol C. Gould and Marx W. Wartofsky, pp. 54–80. New York: Putnam, Capricorn Books.

White, Hayden
- 1972   The Forms of Wildness: Archaeology of an Idea. In *The Wild Man Within: An Image in Western Thought from the Renaissance to Romanticism,* eds. Edward Dudley and Maximillian E. Novak, pp. 3–38. Pittsburgh: University of Pittsburgh Press.

White, Isobel
- 1981   Mrs. Bates and Mr. Brown: An Examination of Rodney Needham's Allegations. *Oceania* 51(3):193–210.

Wilson, Edward O.
- 1978   *On Human Nature.* Cambridge: Harvard University Press.

Winkler, Barbara Scott
- 1980   *Victorian Daughters: The Lives and Feminism of Charlotte Perkins Gilman and Olive Schreiner.* Michigan Occasional Papers in Women's Studies, no. 13 (winter). Ann Arbor: University of Michigan, Women's Studies Program.

Winslow, John Hathaway, and Alfred Meyer
- 1983   The Perpetrator at Piltdown. *Science 83* (September): 32–43.

Wolf, Eric R.
- 1964   *Anthropology.* Englewood Cliffs, New Jersey: Prentice-Hall.

Wollstonecraft, Mary
- 1792   *A Vindication of the Rights of Woman.* Edited by Carol H. Poston. Reprint. New York: Norton, 1975.

Woodward, C. Vann

1981 Spaghetti West. Review of *Land of Savagery, Land of Promise: The European Image of the American Frontier in the Nineteenth Century*, by Ray Allen Billington.*New York Review of Books* (11 June):33–35.

Young, Michael W.
1979 Introduction. In *The Ethnography of Malinowski: The Trobriand Islands, 1915–1918*, ed. Michael W. Young, pp. 1–20. London: Routledge & Kegan Paul.

Young, Philip
1962 The Mother of Us All: Pocahontas Reconsidered. *The Kenyon Review* 24:391–415.

Zihlman, Adrienne L.
1981 Women as Shapers of the Human Adaptation. In *Woman the Gatherer*, ed. Frances Dahlberg, pp. 75–120. New Haven: Yale University Press.

Index

Aboriginal Woman: Sacred and Profane, 47
Alcott, Louisa May, 32
Amazonia: Man and Culture in a Counterfeit Paradise, 78
Amazons, 7, 14, 29, 71–73, 79–86, 88–91, 93–96, 99–102

Bachofen, Johann Jacob, 8–9
Barama River Caribs of British Guiana, The, 89–90
Bates, Daisy, 107n
Beard, Mary Ritter, 35
Beebee, Charles W., 78
Behn, Aphra, 75
Benedict, Ruth, 106n
Biological theories, 13–14
Boas, Franz, 5–6, 26
Bohannan, Paul, 107n
Brazil, 24, 51, 87
Brett, Rev. William H., 78–80
Bridewealth, 42–44, 107n
Butt, Audrey J., 93

Cabral, Pedre Alvarez, 64
Candide, or Optimism, 73–74
Carew, Jan, 78
Carter, Angela, 100
Cavendish, Margaret Lucas, 75
Chagnon, Napoleon A., 52–60, 107n
Chapman, George, 70–71
Columbus, Christopher, 63–64, 71, 93

Coming of Age in Samoa, 26–27, 29, 35
Conrad, Joseph, 31–32, 34
Corentyne Thunder, 91–92

Darwin, Charles, 54, 76–77, 80
de Beauvoir, Simone, 19–20
"De Guiana, Carmen Epicum", 70–71
Description of a New World, Called the Blazing World, The, 75
Discovery of the Large, Rich, and Beautiful Empire of Guiana, The, 69–70
Divale, William Tulio, 25
Division of labor, 14
Donne, John, 68–69
Doyle, Sir Arthur Conan, 84–85
Drayton, Michael, 69
Drummond, Lee, 94
Dworkin, Andrea, 99

El Dorado, 69, 73, 90
Émile, 98
Engels, Frederick, 104n
Evans-Pritchard, E. E., 39–47, 59–60
Evolutionary theory, 7–14, 17

Farabee, William C., 86
Feil, Daryl Keith, 107n
Fieldwork, 4–7, 28, 36, 60, 102
Freeman, Derek, 25–29, 38, 105n

Geography, 64
Gillin, John, 89–90
Gilman, Charlotte Perkins, 10–11
Goodale, Jane C., 48–49, 107n
Green Mansions: A Romance of the Tropical Forest, 82–84
Grimshaw, Beatrice, 31–32
Guppy, Nicholas, 90
Guyana, 68–72, 77, 79–96, 108n

Hall, Joseph, 68
Handful of Dust, A, 88
Harris, Marvin, 25, 53–57, 59–60
Harris, Wilson, 94
Hart, C. W. M., 25, 48–50, 60, 107n
Heart of Darkness, 31
Hegel, Georg Wilhelm, 76
Henfrey, Colin, 91
Henry, Jules, 48
Herland, 10–11
Highland New Guinea, 18–19, 37
Hudson, William Henry, 82–84, 88

Im Thurn, Sir Everard Ferdinand, 72
Indigenous peoples of Africa: Ashanti, 104n; Nuer, 39–47, 50–51, 59–60, 106n–107n
Indigenous peoples of Australia, 25, 30, 47–48, 107n; Tiwi, 25, 39, 47–51, 59–60, 107n; Walbiri, 25
Indigenous peoples of New Guinea, 18–19; Kuma, 37; Mae Enga, 18–19
Indigenous peoples of North America: Iroquois, 11–12, 104n; Pocahontas, 30; Sacagawea, 30
Indigenous peoples of the Pacific: Marquesas Islanders, 29, 31; Samoan Islanders, 25–29, 38; Trobriand Islanders, 33–35; *see* Indigenous peoples of Australia and Indigenous peoples of New Guinea
Indigenous peoples of South America: Akawaio, 93; Arawak, 94; Carib, 78–79, 89–90, 94; Mundurucú, 24, 37; Sharanahua, 37; Wai-Wai, 90; Wapishana, 86; Warrau, 78; Yanomama, 39, 51–60, 107n–108n
Infanticide, 56–57
In the Guiana Forest: Studies of Nature in Relation to the Struggle for Life, 80
In Guiana Wilds: A Study of Two Women, 81

Jungle Peace, 78

Kaberry, Phyllis M., 47, 97
Kemys, Lawrence, 70
King Kong, 85

La Varre, William J., 88–89
Lawrence, D. H., 86–87, 95
Legends and Myths of the Aboriginal Indians of British Guiana, 79–80
Lévi-Strauss, Claude, 44, 100
Lewis, I. M., 107n
Little Women, 32
Lizot, Jacques, 53, 55–58
Locke, John, 61
Lost World, The, 84–85
Lurie, Nancy Oestreich, 97

Male and Female, 14
Malinowski, Bronislaw, 32–35
Manu'a archipelago; *see* Samoa
Marriage, 48–49, 60, 92–93; ghost marriage, 45, 107n; leviratic marriage, 45, 107n; polygyny, 44–45, 48–49, 89–90; woman-marriage, 45–46, 60, 107n
Matriarchy, 7–12, 14, 99–100, 104n
Matriliny, 11, 104n, 106n
Mead, Margaret, 14, 25–29, 35, 105n
Medici, Lorenzo Pietro di, 64
Medicine, Beatrice, 108n
Meggers, Betty J., 78
Meggitt, Mervyn J., 18–19, 25
Melville, Herman, 29, 31

Menstruation, 16–18, 55–56, 105n
Milton, John, 69
Mittelholzer, Edgar, 91–92
Montaigne, Michel de, 66
More, Sir Thomas, 67–68, 74
Morgan, Lewis Henry, 104n
Murphy, Robert F., 24
Murphy, Yolanda, 24

Naipaul, Shiva, 95
Needham, Rodney, 107n
Negro Family in British Guiana, The, 92–93
"New Heaven and Earth", 86–87
New World, 30, 61–70, 73–77, 91, 94, 101, 108n
Norwood, Victor G. C., 90

Ogbu, John U., 107n
Omoo, 29
Orellana, Francisco de, 71
Origin of the Family, Private Property, and the State, The, 104n
Oroonoko; or, the History of the Royal Slave, 75
Outcast of the Islands, An, 34

Palace of the Peacock, 94
Paradise Lost, 69
Parsons, Elsie Clews, 99
Patriarchy, 8–9, 11–13, 99
Participant-observation, 4, 32
Patriliny, 40–42, 60, 106n
Patterns of Culture, 106n
Pilling, Arnold R., 25, 48–50, 60, 107n
Piltdown hoax, 84–85
Poly-Olbion, 69
Polynesia, 25–31, 38
Primitive World and Its Transformations, The 6
Ptolemy, 64

Radcliffe-Brown, A. R., 44, 107n
Raleigh, Sir Walter, 69–70, 72
Ramos, Alcida R., 53, 57, 107n

Rape, 25, 27, 29, 53–55, 59, 62, 67
Rattray, R. S., 104n
Redfield, Robert, 6
Relation of the Second Voyage to Guiana, A, 70
Rich, Adrienne, 19–20
Rodway, James, 80–81
Roth, Walter E., 85
Rousseau, Jean Jacques, 98
Ruddick, Sara, 20

Salter, Elizabeth, 107n
Samoa, 26–29, 38, 51
Sapir, Edward, 106n
Satire III, 68
Satyre IV, 69
Schomburgk, Moritz Richard, 72, 78
Schomburgk, Robert H., 72
Second Sex, The, 19
Second Treatise of Civil Government, The, 61
Sex and Temperament in Three Primitive Societies, 14
Sexual Life of Savages in North-Western Melanesia,The, 35
Shapiro, Judith R., 53, 107n
Shostak, Marjorie, 97
Singer, Alice, 43
Smith, Mary F., 97
Smith, Raymond T., 92–93
Soderini, Piero, 65
Stevenson, Robert Lewis, 26, 28–29
Structural-functionalism, 39, 41, 44
Sudan, 40
Surinam, 75

Thoreau, Henry David, 70
Tiwi Wives, 48
Typee: A Peep at Polynesian Life, 29, 31

Utopia, 67–68

Van Allen, Judith, 104n
Valero, Helena, 107n–108n

Venezuela, 51
Vespucci, Amerigo, 64–66, 68
Victorian women, 7–18, 47, 51, 104n
Vindication of the Rights of Woman, A, 98
Voltaire, François Marie Arouet de, 73–74

Waldseemüller, Martin, 64
Wallace, Alfred, 77
Wanderings in South America, 77–78
Warfare, 56–57, 59–60
Waterton, Charles, 77, 85
Waugh, Evelyn, 87–88
Webber, George Daniel, 79
Wollstonecraft, Mary, 98–99